For Patricia, 16 may 2001,
anniversary of Thomas More's
resignation of the Great Seal,
16. 5. 1532,
G. Marchaolom

PRAYING WITH

SAINT THOMAS MORE

ISBN 2-9511764-1-4
EAN 9782951176416

PRAYING WITH

SAINT THOMAS MORE

Prayers edited by Germain Marc'hadour
and Jocelyne Malhomme

Foreword by Seán Brady, Archbishop of Armagh

ACKNOWLEDGMENTS

In *Moreana* 131-132, Canon Finan evokes the Cork-born Richard O'Sullivan, Q.C. (1878-1963), who founded the Thomas More Society of London, and led the world's lawyers in their petition to have Thomas More canonized. As the martyr declined to support his candidature with a miracle, and while people wondered why an Irishman was the most ardent advocate in an Englishman's cause, O'Sullivan quipped : " *that* is the miracle ! " In 1998 the wonder continues with St. Patrick's College, Maynooth, hosting the biggest ever Congress of the *Amici Thomæ Mori*, and its Chancellor, the Primate of All Ireland, ushering in this collection of More's own prayers and of prayers to him.

Thanks are also due to Marie-Claire Robineau, O.P., who years ago begged for a text to be used in praying *to* Saint Thomas, and who checked on these pages with her double experience of prayer and of Early Tudor English.

Dra. Paloma Castillo, M.D.,took the photo of More's statue by Cubitt Bevis on the Chelsea Embankment, and Vianney Le Rumeur that of Holbein's More between his two editors.

FOREWORD

The Catechism of the Catholic Church (§ 313) quotes St. Thomas More consoling his daughter shortly before his martyrdom with these remarkable words :

> Nothing can come but that that God wills. And I make me very sure that whatsoever that be, seem it never so bad in sight, it shall indeed be the best.

More was absolutely convinced that in all things God works for good for those who love him. In his life he lived the words of the Book of Revelation heroically :

> Be faithful unto death and I will give you the crown of life. He who conquers shall not be hurt by the second death (Rev 2.10-11).

Because he believes that the prayers of the saint are the best mirror of his mind and soul, l'Abbé Germain Marc'hadour has decided to publish *Praying with Saint Thomas More*. It is a collection of prayers composed mostly during the last years of the saint's life. These prayers are coloured by the tribulations of those years but they also reveal his constant exposure to the Bible and to the liturgy of the Church.

St. Thomas More, like every saint, was a man of deep personal prayer. More lived his prayers before he formulated them. Although the prayers in this collection are strongly influenced by the tribulations of More's later years, nevertheless the Editor, himself an internationally famous

Moreana scholar, assures us that they are the product of " a lifetime of praying and many years of conducting the family prayers each evening between supper and bedtime ". L'Abbé Marc'hadour places us all in his debt by this timely publication of *Praying with Saint Thomas More*.

My hope is that readers will not be deterred by the sometimes archaic language from taking up this treasury of prayer and making it their own. It comes from the hand of a master whose life was totally permeated by an atmosphere of prayer. His only surviving letter to his wife Alice was written upon the receipt of news of a fire which had occurred during his absence and had destroyed all their barns and part of their house. It shows once more his marvellous trust in the loving providence of a great and gracious God. It is really inspiring for lay people and clergy alike but especially, I imagine, for married lay faithful. It says :

> I pray you be of good cheer and take all the household with you to Church, and there thank God both for that He hath given us and for that He hath taken from us and for that He hath left us, which if it please Him He can increase when He will, and if it please Him to leave us yet less, at His pleasure be it.

Tolle et Lege ! Rather, *Tolle et Ora* !

+ Seán Brady

INTRODUCTION

An old maxim, *lex orandi lex credendi*, equates prayer and belief : the words you pray reflect the faith you hold. To go one step further, " tell me how you pray, I'll tell you what you are ". More's prayers are the best mirror of his mind and soul, of his inmost self. They reveal his constant exposure to the Bible and the Church liturgy, as well as his docility to the Holy Spirit, which " groaneth for us " (he writes quoting Romans 8.26) " in such wise as no tongue can tell "[1]. This edition uses today's punctuation, but retains archaisms, at times providing the modern form in brackets, for instance *sith* [since] ; note that *very*, which is usually an adjective, means *true* ; *wealth* signifies *well-being*, and *a wealthy life* is *a happy life*.

These prayers were penned mostly during the last stage of More's life, the years when he shared most in his Master's " bitter Passion " (1533-35). The clouds in the spiritual sky of England and Christendom, plus the shadow of the king's displeasure (which " spells death ") explain the dominance of deep, dark hues, where one might expect a lighter tone from the saint called " merry Sir Thomas ". Nevertheless they are not the products of a single season ; More's Autumn of mellow

---

[1] *A Dialogue of Comfort*, p. 22 in volume 12 of *The Complete Works of St. Thomas More*. Henceforth we shall refer to that Yale edition with CW and volume number.

fruitfulness reaps a lifetime of praying and many years of conducting the family prayer each evening between supper and bedtime. William Roper, who was a member of the More household before marrying Margaret, the eldest daughter of his host, is a witness to the paterfamilias acting as pastor of his *ecclesia domestica* :

> As Sir Thomas More's custom was daily, if he were at home, besides his private prayers, with his children to say the seven psalms, litany and suffrages following, so was his guise nightly, before he went to bed, with his wife, children and household, to go to his chapel, and there upon his knees ordinarily to say certain psalms and collects with them (*Life*, p. 25).

Here we see the educator preparing his young charges for their day's work through the recitation of the penitential psalms, called " the fruitful sayings of David " in a commentary by Saint John Fisher (London 1508, and many editions until 1530). We can imagine More explaining the Latin to his 'school' as part of their program, to make sure they understood what they were learning by heart.

These psalms, n°s 6, 31, 37, 50 (*Miserere*), 101, 129 (*De profundis*) and 142 in the numbering of the Latin Bible, were printed as a sequence in the Books of Hours which the faithful used as their liturgical manual, a kind of layperson's breviary. One basic virtue of biblical prayer is to humanize those adolescents, that they " should not be like...an horse and a mule that hath no understanding " (Ps 31.9, repeatedly quoted by More).

A chain of verses More compiled from the Psalter includes the entirety of the longest psalms, 37 and 50, in the penitential sequence (remember that these are 38 and 51 in the Hebrew Bible).

The opening verse of the next penitential psalm (Ps 101) was repeated at least seven times a day, as it introduced the collect of each liturgical hour : " *Domine, exaudi orationem meam, et clamor meus ad te veniat* ". In the *Book of Common Prayer*, this gives " Hear my prayer, O Lord, and let my crying come unto thee ".

The *De profundis* was recited each night by the More household on behalf of the departed souls, because it suggests " the depths " of purgatory, and because of one verse which we shall find in the prayer translated from the Latin of Pico (*CW*1, p. 120/20-22) :

> In strait balance of rigorous judgement
>
> If thou shouldst our sin ponder and weigh,
>
> Who able were to bear thy punishment ?

This clearly echoes " *Si iniquitates observaveris, Domine, Domine quis sustinebit ?* " (Ps 129.3), which was sung as the antiphon to that psalm in the service for the dead ; and that service itself, *Officium defunctorum*, was a regular fixture of the Book of Hours. Another petition always included in funerals was the opening verse of psalm 142 : " *Non intres in judicium cum servo tuo* ". Augustine applied it to his mother Monica in the moving prayer which More englished in the *Confutation* : " Enter not with her into judgement " (*CW*8/373).

Margaret Roper, writing in August 1534 to her stepsister Alice, says she began conversing with their imprisoned father " after our seven psalms and the litany said "[1]. They both clearly knew the whole lengthy sequence by heart. The litany

---

[1] In *The Correspondence of Sir Thomas More*, ed. Elizabeth F. Rogers (Princeton University Press, 1947), p. 515. Henceforth this edition will be referred to as *Rogers*.

survives, to some extent, as " general supplication ", in *The Book of Common Prayer*, and in the detailed 'biddings' of the Easter Vigil, also at ordinations and religious professions, and in the intentions listed at Mass before the offertory. The 'collects' capped the enumerative litany with more inclusive formulas, each encapsulating some major petition : the twelve collects of More's own composing (infra, pp. 49-56) are good examples of the genre. The bedtime family prayer which More conducted in his domestic oratory would no doubt comprise some texts from printed prayer-books, while others were drafted by himself to match the needs or wishes of the household within the context of the place and of the season.

Sir Thomas chose for himself a larger measure of prayer than he decreed for his flock. To quote his son-in-law again, he would " sequester himself from worldly company " in a " new-building " at " a good distance from his mansion house...to occupy himself in prayer and study together " ; and there, on Friday, he spent " his time only in devout prayers and spiritual exercises " (*Life*, pp. 25-26). The choice of Friday means that the focus of his pondering was the Passion of our Saviour ; this prepares us for the autograph line in which he prays for grace " to have continually in mind the passion that Christ suffered for me " (below, p. 39) ; it also explains the quality of his last Tower writing, *The Sadness of Christ*, prompted by his intense agony in 1535, but at the same time the fruit of lifelong rumination.

This exercise in sympathy, or empathy, with his " sweet Saviour " during the darkest hours in Gethsemane, while only one of the apostles was awake — Judas approaching in the darkness to betray Jesus with a kiss — was a tradition of medieval piety : in the Book of Hours, printed at Paris (1530), on which More jotted his personal resolutions[1], the office of Our Lady alternates with hours of the Cross. It is a page *de Cruce* that bears his two requests :

> To walk the narrow way that leadeth to life.
>
> To bear the cross with Christ,

and the next item is entitled *de compassione beatæ Mariæ*. The mother of Jesus was his perfect disciple from before his conception to after his ascension.

THE CHURCH SUFFERING

Recent historians have stressed the persistence of bequests, in the testamentary provisions of the English, for prayers on behalf of the dead. Sir John More, father of the martyr, belongs to a huge 'cloud of witnesses' through his last will, dated " the 26th day of February, the year of our Lord 1526 ". He leaves money to support divinity scholars, one at Oxford one at Cambridge, for seven years, in exchange for them " to pray for my soul, all my wives' souls [he was married four times], and for the souls of my father and mother, King Edward IV, John Leicester, Joan his daughter my grandmother ". The enumeration includes his brother Abel, the husbands of his successive wives, and ends with " all Christian souls ". These are mentioned three more times, for instance where he requests " a yearly obit " in his parish church, St Lawrence Jewry, " during

---

[1] All the interventions in his hand — marginal glosses, underlinings or other responses to the text — are reproduced in *Thomas More's Prayer Book*, edited by Louis Martz and Richard Sylvester (New Haven CT, 1969).

ten years after my decease to pray for my soul and all the souls aforesaid and all Christian souls "[1].

Sir John, a judge in the tribunal called the King's Bench, the highest court in the realm, was not swayed by superstitious usage : he was a lucid investor in the capital of divine mercy made available to all humans through a mediation which is itself a corollary of the mystery called *the communion of saints* in the Church's most ancient creed. The habit of saying " God have mercy on his soul " or " God absolve her soul ", or a similar formula whenever one named a dead person was universal in Christendom, and is far from extinct in Catholic usage. When the Reformers attacked the dogma of purgatory and the very principle of praying for the dead, More rushed to the defence of the immemorial tradition with *A Supplication of Souls* (1529). That SOS is spoken by the inmates of purgatory ; may our brief excerpt from their plea bait you into reading the whole book :

> Send hither your prayer ; send hither your alms before you : so shall we find ease thereof, and yet shall ye find it still. For, as he that lighteth another the candle hath never the less light himself, and he that bloweth the fire for another to warm him doth warm himself also therewith, so surely, good friends, the good that ye send hither before you both greatly refresheth us, and yet is wholly reserved here for you, with our prayers added thereto for your further advantage (CW7/219).

---

[1] " Will of Sir John More ", critically presented by Margaret Hastings in *Essential Articles for the Study of Thomas More*, eds. R. S. Sylvester and G. P. Marc'hadour (Hamden CT, 1977), pp. 101-103.

> And among all your alms, somewhat remember us.
> Our wives there, remember here your husbands.
> Our children there, remember here your parents.
> Our parents there, remember here your children.
> Our husbands there, remember here your wives
> (pp. 223-24).
>
> Now, dear friends, remember how nature and
> Christendom [i.e., our Christian identity] bindeth
> you to remember us...God keep you hence or not
> long here, but bring you shortly to that bliss, to
> which Our Lord's love help you to bring us, and we
> shall set hand to help you thither to us (p. 228).

The adverb *thither* refers, of course, to heaven, where the souls, having emerged from their present crucible, will continue praying for the pilgrim Church on earth, and the suffering Church of purgatory.

In coherence with this appeal on behalf of " all the Christian souls ", More in 1532 ends his epitaph, carved for all parishioners to read in the church of Chelsea, with a plea for himself :

> that he may willingly, for the desire of Christ, die,
> and find death not utterly death to him, but the
> gate of a wealthier [*felicioris*] life, help him (I be-
> seech you, good reader) now with your prayers
> while he liveth, and when he is dead also[1].

---

[1] *The Works of Sir Thomas More in the English Tongue* (London, 1557), p. 1421. The translation may have been made by the editors. The Latin original is on p. 1420.

THE BASIC PRAYERS

Roper does not mention the *Pater noster* and the *Ave Maria* as prayed by More and his charges as they were part of everybody's daily menu. The *Book of Hours* advised their recitation at least seven times a day. The rosary, called "Our Lady's Psalter" (CW9/9), entailed their endless repetition. It was a popular devotion. In Holbein's sketch of 1527, More's daughter Cecily is holding her beads : she looks, behind Margaret's back, at Lady Alice kneeling on her prie-dieu and praying from (one supposes) her *Book of Hours*.

The phrase *a paternoster while* occurs repeatedly in More's prose as a measure of duration (e.g., CW6/71 and 83). London still has a Paternoster Row and an Ave Maria Street. Margaret Roper englished Erasmus' paraphrase of the Lord's Prayer as *The Seven Petitions of the Pater noster* (London, 1524).

Although English translations of the *Pater noster* were available (one was made by More's friend, Dean John Colet), most people said it in Latin. More sometimes leaves some of it untranslated, clearly expecting his readers to understand such lines as *Fiat voluntas tua sicut in cælo et in terra* in his last prayer (below, p. 63), or *Ne nos inducas in tentationem, sed libera nos a malo* (CW12/156). This, however, he had englished earlier in the same book : " the *Pater noster*, wherein we pray for our daily food, and to be preserved from the fall in temptation, and to be delivered from evil " (CW12/20).

A CHAIN FROM THE PSALMS

More's *Imploratio divini auxilii contra tentationem*, " beseeching God's help against temptation ", was gathered out of the Psalter while he was in the Tower. What has come to us ends with Psalm 66 ; the compilation, though incomplete, fills twelve octavo pages (CW13/214-225). *Tribulatio*, one of its keywords (e.g.,215/20, 22 ; 218/30 ; 219/29 ; 223/8, etc.), which also appears frequently in the margins of More's complete Psalter, is balanced with the comfort of hope in a happy ending (e.g., 215/23-24 ; 216/1-4 ; 218/18 ; 219/5, 18, 31 ; 220/29 ; 221/19 ; 222/33 ; 225/12 ; etc.).The selection includes Psalm 26.1, which was, and still is, the motto of More's *alma mater*, Oxford University : *Dominus illuminatio mea, et salus mea : quem timebo ?* (217/25). Also present is a verse which More had quoted twelve years before in his treatise on *The Last Things* : " Cast thy thought into God and he shall nourish thee " (CW1/167), and was to quote at least twice in another Tower catena, using the version popularized by the Roman missal : *Jacta cogitatum tuum in Domino* (CW14/629). He sees it not just as expression of praise and supplication, but as " the very sum of clear and lightsome prophecies " (CW7/182). He also quotes Ps 24.3, " Certainly all they that trust in thee shall not be ashamed " (CW1/93). Its message of trust in God's providence is one of the refrains in More's prison letters.

The Psalter, born within Israel when the chosen people were the true church of God, and daily used by Christ himself " even unto death ", was the staple of More's prayer : he would recite it from his *Book of Hours* like thousands of his fellow Catholics.

From left to right : Elizabeth Daunce, More's second daughter ; Margaret Clements, née Giggs, a cousin More brought up ; Sir John, who died in 1530 ; Anne Cresacre, an orphan who in 1529 married John ; Sir Thomas, whose age, 50, dates the composition ; John, his only son ; his domestic fool Henry Patenson ; Cecily Heron, More's third daughter ; Margaret Roper, alias Meg, his eldest child ; Alice Middleton, his second wife.

His translation of Pico's " interpretation upon this psalm
Conserva me " (Ps 15) runs to ten octavo pages in CW1/94-103 :
" Keep me, good Lord...for I have trusted in thee...I have said
to Our Lord : my God art thou " etc. He drew on the Psalter for
brief invocations, sometimes unenglished, e.g. *In te, Domine,
speravi* from Ps 30 and 70 (CW13/218 and 231), also used by the
Church at the end of the *Te Deum*. The Psalms provide counsels
and assurances : thus Ps 115.15, " Precious is in the sight of
God the death of his saints " (CW12/289).

More can use the *Our Father* even polemically, to prove that
" our Saviour himself not only prayed in mind, but also with
mouth " (CW6/44), and that the pilgrim Church on earth daily
begs God's pardon for her sins (CW5/158, 201 ; CW6/206 ;
CW7/66, 80 ; CW8/960-61). It is not ridiculous to recite the
Pater Noster before a cross, since clearly we address it " to
God " (CW8/150). The words *Fiat voluntas tua* (Mt 6.10) occur
again on the lips of Jesus in the garden (Mt 26.42) and are thus
a refrain of More's meditation on *The Sadness of Christ*
(CW14/175-181, 215, 221). He also points out that " our daily
food [is] one of the petitions of the *Pater noster*, that prayer that
[Christ] himself taught his disciples " (CW12/233).

Other models are provided in the New Testament. One
petition dear to More, " I believe, help my unbelief " (Mk 9.24),
is, says a modern novelist, " the most natural and most human
and most agonizing prayer in the Gospel, and I think it is the
foundation prayer of faith "[1]. More recommends it in his little
Treatise to receive the blessed body of Our Lord, along with other
cries from the heart :

---

[1] Flannery O'Connor as quoted by Bishop Niederauer in the collective
book *Flannery O'Connor and the Christian Mystery* (Provo : Brigham
Young U., 1997), p. 24.

Let say unto him with the father that had the dumb son : " *Credo, Domine, adjuva incredulitatem meam,* I believe, Lord, but help thou my lack of belief " ; and with his blessed apostles : " *Domine, adauge nobis fidem,* Lord, increase faith in us " (Lk 17.5). Let us also with the poor publican, in knowledge of our own unworthiness, say with all meekness of heart : " *Deus, propitius esto mihi peccatori,* Lord God, be merciful to me, sinner that I am " (Lk 18.13). And with the centurion : " *Domine, non sum dignus ut intres sub tectum meum,* Lord, I am not worthy that thou shouldst come into my house " (Mt 8.8)[1].

How to pray

Not content to dictate the seven petitions he wishes present on our lips, the Saviour teaches us how to pray by his example, culminating at Gethsemane : there we see him kneeling and even lying prostrate on the hard ground, trustful despite his Father's seeming deafness, welcoming the comfort of a heavenly mediator, persevering with fervour and intensity. In the context of that agony, More recommends again the use of certain verses : Ps 24.4, " Teach me to do thy will ", and Ps 142.10, " Show me your ways and teach me your paths " (CW14/ 205). On the same page he borrows a line from the litany : " With the Church we must say to God, From blindness

---

[1] CW13/199. More renders the Latin differently in his *Dialogue of Comfort* : " I believe, good Lord, but help thou the lack of my belief...Lord, increase our faith " (CW12/13). The centurion's prayer used to be recited (in Latin) three times before the rite of holy communion. More quotes it also in his *Treatise on the Passion* : " Lord, I am not worthy that thou shouldst enter under my house " (CW13/162).

of heart deliver us, o Lord ! ". More completes his biblical mosaic with echoes from the Psalter and the Song of Songs : " Take my right hand ", and " Lead me along thy path ", and " Draw me in the fragrance of thy Holy Spirit " and (if need be) " Drag me with bridle and bit " (CW14/205).

The main lesson of Christ's agony is perseverance : the Master illustrates his commandment that we pray ceaselessly (Lk 18.1), repeated by Saint Paul to various audiences (Col 4.2 ; 1 Thess 5.17), and practised by the early Church (Acts 12.5). The Vulgate words *sine intermissione* are closely rendered by Mary Basset englishing her grandfather's *De Tristitia Christi* : " Pray must you continually without intermission...Pray doth he bid us, not now and then..., but always without any ceasing " (CW14/1098 and 1122). More explains this request by quoting " Master Gerson ", the 15th century Sorbonne luminary : a pilgrim on his way to Santiago de Compostela, Gerson says, is exposed to distractions, yet his feet show that he is never oblivious of his goal.

More himself lives and moves all the time in a praying atmosphere. His correspondence, both private and public, includes a promise to pray, which explicates what is implicit in the term *bedesman*. His prison letters never lack sentences such as " I pray you all pray for me, and I shall pray for you all ". Whereas Cardinal Wolsey ends his dispatches with " fare you well " (e.g.,*Rogers*, p. 316), all of More's 21 extant letters to him contain a full line of prayer, the most usual formula being " Our Lord long preserve your good Grace in honour and health ". Concrete situations colour his formulas : when Meg Roper is pregnant, the fruit of her womb is recommended to God and his Mother (*Rogers*, p. 302/32).

Gratitude is a mood demonstrated throughout Holy Scripture, and it colours the very name of the Mass :

" *Eucharistia*, which in the Greek tongue signifieth giving of thanks " (CW13/155). The only surviving letter from More to his wife, written upon the news of a fire which had destroyed all their barns with part of their house, leaves it for Alice to handle the situation in his absence, but one firm order from the paterfamilias is thanksgiving to Heaven :

> I pray you be of good cheer and take all the house-
> hold with you to church, and there thank God both
> for that [= what] he hath given us and for that he
> hath taken from us and for that he hath left us,
> which if it please him he can increase when he will,
> and if it please him to leave us yet less, at his
> pleasure be it (*Rogers*, p. 423).

OUR HEAVENLY FRIENDS

Mediæval devotion gave the saints a place which the Reformers were unanimous in denouncing as excessive and near-idolatrous. More, in *A Dialogue concerning Heresies* (1529), defends the principle of recourse to mediators ; he enumerates some of the popular helpers : Loy [Eloy], Dorothy, Roch, Sebastian, Germain (for little children), Valery, Wilgefort, Apolline (for the tooth-ache), Zita, and handles the abuses with humorous tolerance (CW6/227). He justifies the practice of going to their shrines and venerating their relics. He shows that images are more than " laymen's books " ; they have a legit-imate appeal even for the learned : a " well-wrought " figure of the crucified, " near to the quick and to the truth ", has more power than the words *Christus Crucifixus* to stir in our minds " the remembrance of his bitter passion " (CW6/46-47).

More, however, seems to have honoured almost exclusively biblical heroes, from Abraham and Job to the apostles Peter and Paul, " the good publican Zacheus ", the Saviour's sweet friends Martha and Mary, the young disciple who clung to Christ in the garden and was nearly captured (Mk 14.51-52), Saint Stephen the protomartyr, and very specially our Blessed Lady.

Where More says *Our Lord*, he means God, as was the usage of his day. Christ is usually *Our Saviour*. The Holy Trinity looms increasingly large in his writings, as does " the blessed Spirit of Christ ". Characteristically, he embraces the divine persons and the citizens of paradise in one broad vision : in dark hours of trial, he writes, we must look forward to our heavenly home — " the Trinity in his high marvellous majesty, our Saviour in his glorious manhood...with his immaculate mother and all that glorious company calling us there to them " (CW12/315).

The " silly [=blessed] souls " in purgatory are also viewed as a company, and they too call to us with one mighty clamour : we are bound to pray for them, and we can count on them to help us even before they are released from their prison into the joy of heaven (CW7/227 et passim). A double solidarity of nature and grace binds together " all folk spiritual and temporal in this world living, and all good Christian souls departed hence...and all the blessed saints in heaven " (CW9/172) : the Mystical Body of Christ is no idle image in More's spirituality. Christ is with us chiefly as the head of that Body, " and therefore to him must we be joined, and as members of his must we follow him " (CW12/311). He is present in Holy Scripture, but even more so in his Holy Catholic Church, and pre-eminently in the Blessed Sacrament of the Altar : hence More's campaign as champion of the Real Presence in three of his last works, including his unfinished *Treatise on the Passion*, from which we shall quote twelve collects.

A spirit of prayer permeates even More's secular works, and contemplation is given as a basic attitude of his Utopians :

> They think that when, with the help of philosophy, they explore the secrets of nature, they are gratifying not only themselves but the author and maker of nature. They suppose that like other artists he created this beautiful mechanism of the world to be admired[1].

The high point of Christian meditation occurs at the thanksgiving pause which follows holy communion :

> Now have we a special time of prayer, while he that hath made us, he that hath bought us, he whom we have offended, he that shall judge us, he that shall either damn us or save us, is of his great goodness become our guest, and is personally present within us, and that for none other purpose but to be sued unto for pardon, and so thereby to save us. Let us not lose this time...Let us say with his two disciples that were going to the castle of Emmaus : " *Mane nobiscum, Domine*, tarry with us, good Lord ! " (CW13/202).

All the prayers collected here, except for the stanzas born of Pico's *deprecatoria*, were published posthumously. They first appeared in print in 1557, thanks to a turn of events which in 1535 was unpredictable. " The Lady Mary ", as the former princess of Wales had been labelled since the 1534 Act of Parliament excluding her from succession as the fruit of an incestuous marriage, had to be re-legitimized and to become

---

[1] *Utopia : Latin Text and English Translation*, ed. by George M. Logan, Robert M. Adams & Clarence H. Miller (Cambridge U P, 1995), p. 183.

Queen Mary I before official censorship would grant the imprimatur for the prose of convicted traitors. As More was penning his last prayer, at the risk of being interrupted by the king's envoy coming to fetch him for execution, he could hardly have imagined that within a quarter century it would appear in a handsome folio volume dedicated to England's Catholic sovereign (then officially a bastard) ; that it would be studied and annotated by a Protestant scholar for a critical edition in a secular university of the (still semi-fabulous) New World ; that it would be translated into the exotic languages of countries almost as shadowy in 1535 as his own Isle of Nowhere ; that some of its paragraphs would be recited as collects at masses celebrated in commemoration of him and of Bishop Fisher, who had shed his blood on the previous June 22nd, the feast of Saint Alban, the Roman legionary, Britain's protomartyr.

More knew, however, that the ways of Providence can exceed the loftiest flights of man's imagination, for " nothing is impossible to God " : Gabriel's final words to the Virgin (Lk 1.37) were repeatedly echoed in More's defence of the faith (CW7/243, CW8/77 ; CW11/63).

GOD'S LOVE AFFAIR WITH MAN

More, without perhaps being a mystic, does not overlook the intimate love affair between God and each human soul. Leafing through the Book of Revelation, which he calls Apocalypse, he pauses, not at the double-edged sword or the terrifying horses, but at the highly personal invitations. Two verses will serve as samples of his reading. One is 3.20, which Holman Hunt illustrated so tellingly in " The Light of the World ". More quotes it seven times to demonstrate that, although God " loved us first ", he will not intrude into the sanctuary of our souls, he will beg admission. This is More's version : " Lo I stand at the door knocking ; if any man hear my voice and open me the door, I will go in to him, and sup with him, and he with me " (*CW*11/85). He comments : " God would not so often and so earnestly call and cry upon us, nor stand and knock at the door of our heart, if ourself could nothing do to the opening thereof, and thereby to let him in " (*CW*8/787). So there is no doubt, he concludes, that the human will is free, and that God, who made us without us, will not save us without us ; let us remember, as we call on God, that he himself stands as a beggar at our door.

Verse 2.17 is quoted, in *A Dialogue of Comfort*, by Uncle Antony, who seems to be playing on the name of his young interlocutor, alluding to his name, Vincent : " *Vincenti dabo manna absconditum, et dabo illi calculum candidum, et in calculo nomen novum scriptum, quod nemo scit nisi qui accipit*. To him that overcometh will I give manna secret and hid ; and I will give him a white suffrage, and in his suffrage a new name written, which no man knoweth but he that receiveth it " (*CW*12/309). More explains that " in Greece, where Saint John did write,...they used round stones to choose and elect men " [= humans] : that is how the white pebble bearing the name of God's own " candidate " came to be called *suffrage* in More's translation. Each person receives that confidential " nomination ", yet remains free to accept or refuse the 'room' to which this election entitles them in the Father's mansion.

" YOUR MOST BOUNDEN BEDESMAN "

More's signature is often preceded by that formula, which means " under obligation to pray for you ". Instead of *bedesman*, he sometimes uses *bedeman/beedman* : the root is the same as in *bidding*, or the German *beten*, " to pray ". Meg utilizes the same words in the feminine when she signs herself " your most obedient daughter and *bedeswoman* Margaret Roper, which daily and hourly is *bounden* to pray for you " (*Rogers*, p. 539). The inmates of almshouses and colleges, owing a daily debt of prayer to the benefactors who had endowed those institutions, were the founders' *bounden bedesfolk*. The persons to be specially prayed for were listed on a *bederoll* (CW7/115.13). Lady Alice More, in a letter to Henry VIII, describes as " your most humble subjects and continual bedefolk " the family of his " subject and *bedeman* Sir Thomas More " (*Rogers*, p. 547) ; like Meg, she makes the meaning of the term explicit : " all your said poor bedefolk shall daily during their lives pray to God for the preservation of your most royal estate " (p. 549). A letter to Cromwell in which she also pledges to pray for him, is signed " By your poor continual *oratrix* " (*Rogers*, p. 555). The word, from Latin *orare*, " to pray ", may have been suggested by the more learned members of her household. The first meaning of *orator* had been spokesman (for instance ambassador), which fitted it for a prayerful intercession or supplication. More too had included his family in a pledge of prayer for Cardinal Wolsey after his appointment as *Speaker* : (*Rogers*, p. 278).

> I and all mine, as the manifold goodness of your Grace hath already bound us, shall be daily more and more bounden to pray for your Grace, whom Our Lord long preserve in honour and health.
> Your humble orator and most bounden beedsman,

MORE'S *PRAYER BOOK* IN CONTEXT

The label *Book of Hours*, nearly vanished out of usage since Vatican II, has just been revived by Sean Finnegan in a compilation (The Canterbury Press) with a foreword by Graham Leonard, emeritus bishop of London (and now a Catholic priest). As for *Prayer Book*, it has tended to designate the Anglican *Book of Common Prayer*, published by Archbishop Cranmer in 1549, revised in 1552 under Edward VI (when the word *Mass* disappeared), under Elizabeth (1559), under James I (1604), and finally after Cromwell's Commonwealth (1662).

Hours meant the canonical " hours " of the day, from Lauds at dawn to Compline at bedtime. One fixture that survived in modern missals for the faithful is a calendar of the feasts. Each Gospel was sampled through a one page extract : usually the prologue to John, the Annunciation from Luke, the Nativity according to Matthew, and Christ's farewell in the last chapter of Mark. A full narrative of the Passion preceded the Office of Our Lady. Each Hour was followed by a shorter commemoration " of the cross ", and sometimes another " of the Holy Spirit — *de Spiritu sancto* ". The day ended with the *Salve Regina*. Then came the Seven Penitential Psalms and the Office for the Dead, *vigiliæ mortuorum* : the word *Dirge* in English derived from the beginning of the first antiphon to Matins, *Dirige, Domine*. The saints were content with a collect each, the length of which could vary according to their local importance. The book usually ended with a number of prayers, each introduced by a vernacular rubric specifying the intention or occasion for instance, " at the levacioun of our Lord ", " when thou receivest the sacrament ", and sometimes the rate of the indulgence attached to the " devout recitation ".

WADING THROUGH MORE'S *PRAYER BOOK*

The manual acquired in 1965 by Yale University is the more unique as it is made up of two books bound under one cover. Though both printed in Paris, they came out of different presses in different years, and More's autographs belong to a double script : a Gothic kind of hand for English, and italic for Latin. Both are incomplete, for whatever reason ; the omissions may have occurred when the two books were bound together, so as to make the volume less bulky, and thus handier. The " godly meditation " in the *Horæ* looks complete, with a final paragraph that winds it up on the 19th page, at the end of Sext. The *imploratio ex psalmis*, which is not known to have survived in More's hand, ends abruptly with verses drawn from Psalm 66. Why ? Not because More's interest had waned at the point, since he quotes Ps 67.7 (about unanimity in the house of God) more often than any other verse from the Old Testament, while 67.1 is the example he singles out to recommend vigorous imprecations : " Special verses may there be drawn out of the Psalter ", says his Uncle Antony, " against the devils' [or devil's : apostrophes had not yet come into use] wicked temptations, as for example *Exsurgat Deus et dissipentur inimici ejus* " (CW12/156). Saint Athanasius had already exhorted his flock to use that exorcism.

The *Dialogue of Comfort against Tribulation* abounds in verses either copied by More or carrying some response from his pen : *tribulatio* appears in 27 of the 150 marginal notes. The dialogue is located in a Hungary besieged by the Moslem Ottomans, and the *Turks* are evoked in six of the glosses ; they head an invitation to give thanks at the beginning of Psalm 84 : " After victory, either against the Turks or against the demons in temptation ; or a thanksgiving after the plague, or drought, or a spell of rainy weather have been taken away " (fol. lxvj verso, Yale facsimile p. 140).

The concerns of an entire population are voiced in those lines. The preceding psalm (83) is more personal, and inspires this heading : " The prayer either of a man who is shut up in prison, or of one who lies sick in bed, yearning [to go] to church, or of any faithful man who yearns for heaven ". Its title, *Quam dilecta tabernacula*, and the *altaria* of verse 4 evoke the Eucharist, which (in Newman's words) is " God's presence and his very self/And essence all divine ". The Tower precincts included two places of worship, St. Peter-in-Chains and St. John's, where Mass was said each day, and the consecrated species preserved round the clock. As Fisher and More were deprived of communion, one can imagine how their hearts would turn longingly toward the Blessed Sacrament, which had been the final theme of their polemics in defense of the Catholic faith : Fisher's in *De veritate corporis* against Œcolampadius, and More's with his *Answer* to a Zwinglian tract (*CW*11). More pursued the topic in 1534, when he could no longer publish, with *How to receive the Blessed Body of Our Lord* and *A Treatise upon the Passion*.

" Yearning for heaven " qualifies the pious pilgrim of Ps 83.7 plodding in *valle lacrymarum*, " in this vale of misery in this time of tears ", says More (*CW*11/33), or " in this time of tears, this vale of misery, this simple wretched world " (*Rogers*, p. 519). The phrase *in hac lacrymarum valle*, in the *Salve Regina*, had further orchestrated the mood of exiled children of Eve heading for their heavenly home.

Other psalms sing of hope and trust : *fiducia* appears 8 *times* in the margin. *Gratitude* is voiced for diverse favours : *pro consolatione, de liberatione a tribulatione vel tentatione*, etc. The record number of references is to the devils with *diabolus* thrice and *demon/demones* 40 times, in plural or singular depending on the context : the main reason for their ubiquity is not fear, but diverting the curses away from human foes (whom he prays to view as his " best friends " — see p. 39/line 35) to those invisible powers of darkness (Eph 6.12) explicitly exorcised in More's *Dialogue of Comfort* (CW12/101, 317) and *De Tristitia Christi* (CW14/545).

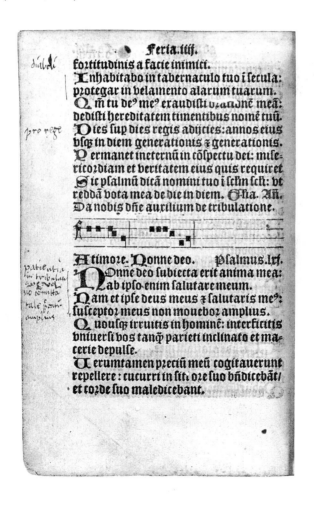

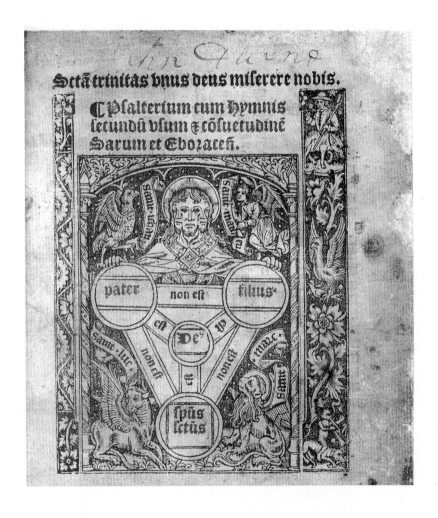

The equality of the three Persons — *egal*, says More in Law French — is stressed in this title-page of the book (Paris, 1522) on which he jotted some 150 notes and many marks. That edition, being geared at the English market, follows the usage of Salisbury (Sarum) and York (Eboracensem), but the evangelists retain their French names. *Deus* and *Spiritus sanctus* are spelt with the usual contractions.

The Holy Trinity was especially honoured in England : Saint Thomas Becket, having been ordained at Canterbury on the Octave Day of Pentecost (1162), decreed that, in his diocese, that first Sunday of ordinary time would be dedicated to the Most Blessed Trinity and the feast was gradually extended to the whole Church.

Our woodcut evidences the universality of the devotion, as does Pico's highly Trinitarian prayer translated by More (see p. 74 infra). Over the years, the Three Persons loom larger and larger in More's writings, quite perceptibly in the correspondence of his last years : see, for instance, the valedictory formula in his letters to Cromwell (*Rogers*, p. 488 and 500), Henry VIII (p. 491), Meg Roper (p. 547). Writing to Antonio Bonvisi (p. 561 and 563), More seems to delight in expatiating on each Person's titles ; this is Elizabeth Mc Cutcheon's translation of his Latin : " with God the Father unbegotten, and his only-begotten Son, our Lord and Redeemer Jesus-Christ, and the Holy Spirit of them both, the Comforter proceeding from them both, we shall fully enjoy eternal joy " (*Moreana* 71-72, 56/56-58). His *Dialogue of Comfort* conjures up an image of heaven as a family : " the Trinity in his high marvellous majesty, our Saviour in his glorious manhood...with his immaculate Mother and all that glorious company calling us there to them " (CW12/315).

The Body in Prayer

Against the Reformers' hostility to physical expressions of worship, More evokes such spectacular examples as David's dancing " to God's honour " (*CW6/44, CW7/33, CW8/163f.*) and Magdalen's multiple homage to the body of Jesus, culminating with the " poundweight of ointment " she poured upon his head (*CW13/76f.*) : the enemies of devotional gestures found themselves kin with David's Puritan wife and with Judas, " the covetous wretch ", " grudging " (also Chaucer's word) at Magdalen's unthrifty waste of precious nard (*CW6/79, CW7/33-34 and 58, CW8/699, CW13/76-80*).

Liturgical dancing had disappeared, and so had prostration, which clearly appealed to More. In Utopia's temples, as soon as the priest appears in his vestments, " all the people fall on the ground in veneration : *in terram venerabundi procumbunt* " and remain in that position until invited to rise ; they prostrate themselves again at the close of the service (*CW4/234-36*).

The Old Testament provided models for that posture : when Ezra read the Law, the people " worshipped the Lord with their faces to the ground " (Neh 8.6), and " all the people fell on their faces in adoration " when the altar was rededicated (1 Mac 4.55). More is not advocating for England such collective demonstration, but, at a personal level, he is drawn to imitate the Jesus of Gethsemane, lying flat on the bare ground, revering his heavenly Father with a gesture which no tyrant would dare demand from his subjects (*CW14/111-15, 147*). Let us seek for each other, he writes to Meg, the grace " in all our agonies and troubles devoutly to resort *prostrate* unto the remembrance of that bitter agony which our Saviour suffered, before his Passion, at the Mount " (*Rogers*, p. 509).

For people less ready to imitate Christ, he still hopes that " contemplating our captain flat on the ground " will make them ashamed of their negligence when they pray strolling, or sitting on a stool, or kneeling on a single knee, or else with a cushion under their knees, if not also under their elbows (CW14/124-27). He must, when he wrote this, have been thinking of Lady Alice as Holbein represents her in the sketch of the Chelsea family, with the two cushions quite visible on her prie-dieu. A sentence in German near her figure says " This one should sit " : one can imagine the *paterfamilias* suggesting the change, no doubt on the teasing tone with which Erasmus says he governed his household. However high he placed the ideal (as we know from *Utopia*), More was indulgent in practice. He probably would not frown on the hassocks which the ladies of the parish have made for the Old Church at Chelsea, embroidering quite a few with patterns related to the More family : he would object if the embroidered kneelers featured, for instance, a cross or a chalice, as that would entail disrespect to Christ's person via the symbols of his Passion or his Eucharist.

More's coat of arms featuring the rebus of three moorcocks : embroidered kneelers in Chelsea Old Church.

After commenting on the Saviour's prostration, More makes it clear that he forbids no-one " to pray while walking or sitting or even lying down. Indeed I wish that, whatever our bodies may be doing, we would at the same time lift up our minds to God " (CW14/135). The Jewish prophet, not content to remember God while in bed (Ps 118.62), would rise at midnight to praise him (Ps 62.7), and More suggests that we follow suit (CW14/7-9, 137).

Saint Mary Magdalen, who received Christ's praise for breaking her flask of costly nard, was a great favourite of More's. She is forever the model contemplative : our picture is part of an Entombment of Christ at St. Peter's Benedictine Abbey, Solesmes ; it was carved by Michel Colombe in 1496, the year Thomas More began his legal studies at Lincoln's Inn. A decade earlier (15.X.1486), Pico had quoted an advice which his translator More was to follow : " I desire you not so to embrace Martha [=*vita activa*] that you should utterly forsake Mary " (CW1/86.17-8).

In Luke 11.39, Mary sits at the feet of Jesus drinking in his every word. Martha complains that her sister leaves her alone to wait upon the guests. Though he has chosen action by marrying and entering public life, More often defends the priorities of contemplation by evoking the scene at Bethany with

> Mary Maudlin, whose idle sitting at her ease and hearkening [Our Saviour Christ] accounted and declared for better business than the busy stirring and walking about of his good hostess Martha, which was yet of all worldly business occupied about the best, for she was busy about alms and hospitality, and the guesting of the best poor man and most gracious guest that ever was guested in this world (CW12/185, CW13/201, CW15/301).

Eus in adiutoriū meum intende.
Dñe ad adiuuādum me festina.
Gloria patri et filio : et spū sctō.
Sicut erat in prin.&c. Hymnus.
Sax.   c ij

to sett the world at nonght

A GODLY MEDITATION

The term *meditation* was aptly chosen by the 1557 editors of More's *English Works*, since the list of sentences in the infinitive constitutes a program which More sets out to achieve, with God's grace : *meditari*, in classical Latin, means to envisage, to plan, even to plot (for example in *CW4/78.4*).

Why did More jot down his resolutions in the margins of his prayer book ? He may have penned them at a time when he lacked paper : one prison letter ends abruptly " for lack of paper " (*Rogers*, p. 507). The *Book of Hours* or *Horæ beatæ Mariæ* on which he wrote was printed at Paris in 1530 ; the copy bearing his autograph additions on 19 successive pages is now in the Beinecke Library of Yale University.

Why did he begin his jottings on folio xvii ? They coincide with the daytime Hours of Our Lady's Office, which alternate with those of the Cross. Garry Haupt perceived " a very fluid but unmistakable relationship between the prayers and the *Prayer Book* " (CW13/clxvii) : I am not aware of it.

The traditional woodcut for Prime was the Nativity. On the left, see the saddle which " bore the most blessed burden that was ever born " — Jesus in the womb of Mary. *Sar* underneath the text (for Sarum) shows that the edition was geared at the English market, which followed the use of Salisbury. More's " Give me thy grace ", in the top margin makes the meditation clearly a prayer.

1.   Give me thy grace, good Lord,
2.   To set the world at nought,
3.   To set my mind fast upon thee,
4.   And not to hang upon the blast of men's mouths.
5.   To be content to be solitary,
6.   Not to long for worldly company,
7.   Little and little utterly to cast off the world,
8.   And rid my mind of all the business thereof.
9.   Not to long to hear of any worldly things,
10. But that the hearing of worldly phantasies may be to me displeasant.
11. Gladly to be thinking of God,
12. Piteously to call for his help,
13. To lean unto the comfort of God,
14. Busily to labour to love him.
15. To know mine own vility and wretchedness,
16. To humble and meeken myself under the mighty hand of God,
17. To bewail my sins passed,
18. For the purging of them, patiently to suffer adversity.
19. Gladly to bear my purgatory here,
20. To be joyful of tribulations,
21. To walk the narrow way that leadeth to life,
22. To bear the cross with Christ.

23. To have the last thing in remembrance,

24. To have ever afore mine eye my death that is ever at hand,

25. To make death no stranger to me.

26. To foresee and consider the everlasting fire of hell,

27. To pray for pardon before the judge come.

28. To have continually in mind the passion that Christ suffered for me,

29. For his benefits uncessantly to give him thanks.

30. To buy the time again that I before have lost.

31. To abstain from vain confabulations,

32. To eschew light foolish mirth and gladness,

33. Recreations not necessary / to cut off.

34. Of worldly substance, friends, liberty, life and all, to set the loss at right nought, for the winning of Christ.

35. To think my most enemies my best friends, for the brethren of Joseph could never have done him so much good with their love and favour as they did him with their malice and hatred.

36. These minds are more to be desired of every man, than all the treasure of all the princes and kings, Christian and heathen, were it gathered and laid together all upon one heap.

NOTES TO THE LINES

1.   good Lord

More's *good Lord*, used four times in his prayer from Pico, and another four times in his collects, punctuates his devout prayer with a dozen occurrences, once expanded to " good gracious Lord ".

2.   set the world at nought

This *contemptus mundi* may sound an unduly negative response to creation, especially in a humanist who loved life and people. Yet it coheres with the pejorative sense given to *the world* in the New Testament, especially St. John's gospel ; 1 Jn 5.19 describes this fallen and unredeemed world as " all set in malice " (CW6/376), and St. Paul, in respect of our heavenly inheritance, " reputed all other things for dung " (Phil 3.8, as quoted in CW1/100) ; " the world ", its " busyness " or agitation, and its " phantasies " (lines 7 to 10) amplify this purpose of unworldliness.

4.   not to hang upon the blast

The image is that of riding a flimsy unsubstantial vector. The word *blast*, as the noun corresponding to *blow*, designates the breeze of flattery no less than the squalls of rebuke or insult : Pico warns his young correspondent against " the pestilent blast of vainglory, ...the vain promotion of a little popular fame " as well as against the backbiters : " Let them ball, let them bark, go thou boldly forth " (CW1/90-91).

5.   content to be solitary

More's cruellest ordeal was not to be shut up in the 'strait room' of his prison cell (he had practised and welcomed that kind of solitude), but for him, the companionable commoner, to look odd and 'singular' in his opposition to the will of his 'natural lord' the king. He also confesses to Meg his yearning to " talk with my friends, and specially my wife and you that pertain to my charge " (*Rogers*, p. 543).

11.   Gladly to be thinking

This participial construction, rare in Tudor English, suggests something one goes about with deliberation and continuity. *Gladly* here, and at petition n° 19, might echo Chaucer's famous line about the clerk of Oxford : " Gladly would he learn, and gladly teach ".

13.   To lean unto

To lean unto may sound archaic. More himself uses *upon* where uncle Antony, in *A Dialogue of Comfort*, won't be reckoned his kinsfolk's chief comfort : to lean upon him, rather than on God, would be to " lean upon a rotten reed " (CW12/5).

14.   Busily to labour to love

Human affection may be a sweet feeling, but the love of God can be (as Dorothy Day was to recall in a book's title) " a harsh and dreadful thing ", the fruit of man's generous, sacrificial response to God's initiative. Godliness entails training : it is a conquest born of strenuous exercise (1 Tim 4.7).

16.   To humble and meeken myself

Humble and *meek* are near synonyms — here, as in Mt 11.29 where Jesus describes himself as " meek and humble " ; *the mighty hand of God* echoes 1 Pet 5.6.

17-20. For the purging...tribulations

Sin being like a stain, or the dross encasing precious ore, adversity is the crucible or the detergent. " Nothing unclean or polluted will enter " into the heavenly City (Rev 21.27) : hence the need for purgatory, and the wish, already proverbial in More's age, to be cleansed while on earth. The popular *Jesus Psalter* made its users repeat ten times : " Send me here my purgatory ". John Fisher recommends the prayer " Good Lord, punish me in this life " (*Works, EETS,* p. 41). Among the virtues of tribulation, Antony notes that it " helpeth to purge our sins passed " and " much [di]minisheth our pains in purgatory " (*CW*12/75). More agrees with his fictional spokesman when he says to Meg Roper that God's 'high goodness' shall make his imprisonment " serve for release of my pain in purgatory " (*Rogers*, p. 531).

21.   To walk the narrow way

The proverbial 'narrow way' stems from Christ's own words in Mt 7.13-14 and Lk 13.24. As early as 1506, More writes that even the sages of pre-Christian Greece chose that strait path (*CW*3/Pt1, p. 4). Pico, as englished by More, urges his nephew " to enter by the strait gate that leadeth to heaven " (*CW*1/82).

22.   To bear the cross

More's autograph shows that he began with " To bear my ", then struck off *my* before proceeding with *the*, perhaps to imply that the *via crucis* is a universal highroad, the king's way for all the followers of Christ. " Take up *the* cross " is a familiar phrase, and the Greek *ho stauros*, " **the** cross ", is frequent in Scripture (Mt 27.40, 42 ; Mk 15.30 ; Lk 23.26 ; Jn 19.19, 31 ; 1 Cor 1.18 ; Gal 5.11 ; Eph 2.16).

23-25. To have the last thing...

The noun *thing* should be read as a plural, like other Saxon monosyllables which in Tudor English remained invariable. More's treatise on *The Last Things*, if finished, would, after death, have pondered doom (or judgement), hell and heaven. It was a major theme of meditation in the 15th and 16th centuries. The familiar motto *memento mori*, " remember death ", was (in jest) also quoted as meaning " remember More ". Pico's fifth " weapon of spiritual battle " urges the soldier of Christ to consider that " Death stealeth on full slyly and unaware, / He lieth at hand " (CW1/111). The *Imitation of Christ,* which More recommended, devotes a chapter (I/23) to " Meditation of death ", with this beatitude : " Blissful is he that hath the hour of his death ever before his eyen ".

26-27. To foresee and consider...

Judgement and hell are next in the four last things. Heaven has been evoked in the " glad thinking of God " and the eternal life at the end of " the narrow way " (lines 11 and 21). But the darker alternative needs pondering in a meditation geared at the achievement of an ascetic discipline. More reminded the king's commissioners that, in his options, " the difference standeth between heading [=beheading] and hell " (*Rogers*, p. 538).

28.   the passion that Christ suffered for me

To the priest Nicolas Wilson, his fellow prisoner, More wrote : " I have a long reckoning and a great to give account for, but I put my trust in God, and in the merits of his bitter Passion " (*Rogers*, p. 537). Here the layman, addressing a doctor of divinity, does not shrink from evoking the Passion of **God** ! He was penning a meditation on the first (and perhaps worst) stage of his master's Passion, when Christ was sweating blood in the Garden from anguish and fear (CW14/189, 227). To Cromwell and the king's councillors, he said he had determined " that my whole study should be upon the Passion of Christ and mine own passage out of this world " (*Rogers*, p. 552) : *passage* alludes to death as a paschal *transitus* toward the promised Land through the Red Sea of Christ's blood.

29. uncessantly to give him thanks

If prayer needs to be unceasing, it should be so especially in its highest expression : gratitude. Saint Paul, among others, gives an example (1 Cor 1.14 ; Phil 1.3-4 ; 1 Thess 2.13). More reminds us that " *Eucharistia*...in the Greek tongue signifieth giving of thanks " (CW13/155).

33. Recreations not necessary / to cut off.

The slanting bar is the only sign of punctuation in the whole litany of resolutions. In More's household, as in Utopia, idleness was discouraged, and the games themselves had a purpose. Yet this very request implies that some recreation *is* necessary. In *A Dialogue of Comfort*, a whole chapter is devoted to " worldly recreations " : Antony agrees with More as portrayed in Roper's *Life*, " let them serve us but for sauce, and make them not our meat " (CW12/84). More was in a darker mood in 1533 when, refuting a heretical *Supper of the Lord*, he inveighed against the slothful who " live either in idleness or in idle busyness " and the gamesters for " driving forth all their days in gaming. God sent men hither to wake and work, and as for sleep and gaming (if any gaming be good in this vale of misery in this time of tears), it must serve but for a refreshing of the weary and forwatched body, to renew it unto watch and labour again...For rest and recreation should be but as a sauce " (CW11/33). The phrase *vale of misery* (or of tears), echoing the *vallis lacrymarum* in Ps 83.7 and the *Salve Regina*, occurs in at least four other works of More (*CW1*/346 ; *CW8*/65 ; *CW12*/41 ; *Rogers* p. 519) and in Roper's *Life* (81/4-7).

34.   for the winning of Christ.

More is no ascetic, no Stoic. His discipline of detachment from everything has a mystical intent, as did that of St. Paul, when he reputed all his human assets " for dung ", says More, englishing the Vulgate *stercora* (Phil 3.8) that he might win Christ (*CW1*/100).

35.   To think my most enemies...

Joseph himself took his brothers to witness that their hostility had served the purpose of God's providence (Gen 45.5). Both the Roman breviary (on 22 June) and the *Catechism of the Catholic Church* (§ 313) quote the famous sentence in which More expressed his optimism :

> Nothing can come but that that [= which] God will[s], and I make me very sure that, whatsoever that be, seem it never so bad in sight, it shall indeed be the best " (*Rogers*, p. 531-32).

Joseph sold by his brothers, from a Prayer-Book of More's time.

Ad sextam de cruce

In the traditional Book of Hours, each Hour of the Virgin is followed by a one-page Hour of the Cross. Our woodcut was reproduced in *Moreana* n°5 (February 1965), then in *Thomas More's Prayer Book* (1969, p. 20), before serving as a frontispiece to *CW*13. It represents the *via crucis*, which took place around noon, *sextam horam*, that is the sixth hour of the day (Mt 20.5 ; Mk 15.33 ; Lk 23.44 ; Jn 19.14). Christ, on his way to Calvary, is helped by Simon of Cyrene, and seems to be turning his face toward his Mother. The poem beside the medallion evokes Jesus' crucifixion, between two thieves, and his thirst quenched with gall : " the Lamb washes our sin by suffering derision ". The *Oratio* was the same at each Hour of the Cross, and repetition printed it into the users' memory. Thomas Bilney prayed it before receiving his last communion, More tells us, and repeated the words *ecclesiæ tuæ pacem and concordiam* " divers times...with tunsions [beatings] upon his breast " in sorrow for disturbing that " peace and concord of the Church " (*CW*8/25). The text was often printed in Tudor English. We offer a modern translation :

> Lord Jesus Christ, son of the living God, put your passion, cross and death between your judgment and our souls now and at the hour of our death ; vouchsafe to bestow mercy and grace on the living, rest and pardon on the dead, peace and concord on your Church, and on us sinners everlasting life and glory, you who with the Father and the Holy Spirit live and reign, God, forever and ever. Amen.

Ad sextam de cruce.

Hora sexta ie¬
sus est cruci con
clauatus. Atq3 cum
latronibus pendens
deputatus. Pre tor¬
mentis sitiens felle
saturatus. Agn9 cri
men diluit sic ludifi¬
catus. V9. Adoram9
te christe: et benedici
mus tibi. R3. Quia
per sanctam crucem
tuam redemisti mū¬
dum. Oremus.   Oratio.

DOmine iesu christe fi'i dei viut: pone
passionē crucē et mortē tuā inter iu¬
diciū tuū & aīas nostras nunc & in hora mor
tisnostre:et largiri digneris viuis misericor
diā et gratiā/defunctis requiē et veniā / ec¬
clesie tue pacē et concordiā / et nobis pctōri¬
busvītā & gloriā sempiternā. Qui cū patre
et spū sancto viuis et regnas deus. Per oīa
secula seculor. Amē. Gloriosa passio dūi no
stri iesu xpī eruat nos a dolore tristi / & pdu
cat nos ad gaudia paradisi. Amē. Pater no¬
ster. Aue maria gratia.

This collect is followed by a formula which ends every Hour of the Cross, and is made easier to memorize through rather crude rhymes :

> *Gloriosa passio Domini nostri Jesu Christi*
> *eruat nos a dolore tristi,*
> *et perducat nos ad gaudia paradisi. Amen.*

> May the glorious passion of Our Lord Jesus Christ
> wrench us from sad sorrow,
> and lead us all the way to the joys of paradise. Amen

Sext ends on the facing page with a brief *De compassione beatæ Mariæ*, leaving good space for the concluding lines of More's meditation. These last two pages feature more corrections than the previous seventeen : one is the use, as an afterthought, of the conjunction *for* to link the top and the bottom margins into one sentence. One emendation in heavy ink in the final entry seems to be by another hand.

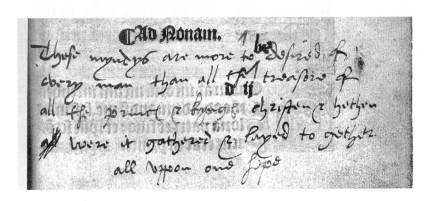

TWELVE COLLECTS

The *oratio* we encountered at the close of Sext is labelled a *collect* in More's *Confutation* (CW8/25), a term still used by the Catholics, and even more so in the Church of England, to designate a prayer which 'collects' a major intention of the liturgy into one recapitulative sentence. The comprehensive capsule can become fairly lengthy as it includes a whereas or two. More himself composed a dozen collects in *A Treatise upon the Passion*, each wrapping up the 'points' of sacred history he had been exposing. The whole sentence can be read in public recitation, as long as the articulations are allowed to stand out and lay the structure bare ; they consist usually of *so* or *such* balanced in the subordinate clause by *as* or/and *that*.

1. CREATION AND FALL OF THE ANGELS (p. 11)

The first collect (CW13/11) is the distillation of six pages about the creation and fall of the angels. It begins with two relative clauses, hinged clearly on *whose* and *whom* ; the main clause, quite brief, is followed by a cascade in which *that* plays two functions.

> O glorious blessed Trinity, whose justice hath damned unto perpetual pain many proud rebellious angels, whom thy goodness had created to be partners of thy eternal glory, for thy tender mercy plant into mine heart such meekness that I so may, by thy grace, follow the motion of my

good angel, and so resist the proud suggestions of those spiteful spirits that fell, as I may through the merits of thy bitter Passion be partner of thy bliss with those spirits that stood, and now confirmed by thy grace in glory shall stand for ever.

The grammatical hooks and handles which make this collect graspable are complemented by the opposition between the rebellious angels that *fell* and the good angels that *stood*, a contrast More had encountered in, for instance, Rom 14.4 : " Every man *suo domino stat et cadit* " (*Rogers*, p.559), and 1 Cor 10.12 : " He that thinketh that he standeth, let him beware he fall not " (CW8/430). Notice that More, as in the Pico prayer, speaks to the triune God of " thy bitter passion ". And remember that *wealth* (in the second collect) means happiness :

2. CREATION AND FALL OF MANKIND (p. 24-25)

Almighty God, that of thine infinite goodness didst create our first parents in the state of innocency, with present wealth and hope of heaven to come, till through the devil's train their folly fell by sin to wretchedness, for thy tender pity of that Passion that was paid for their and our redemption, assist me so with thy gracious help that unto the subtle suggestions of the Serpent I never so incline the ears of mine heart, but that my reason may resist them, and master my sensuality, and refrain me from them.

Saint Thomas More (1477-1535)

The things, good Lord, that I pray for,
Give me the grace to labor for.

(Thomas More's last prayer)

Imprimerie Mollé Angers

¶ A prayer.

Almightye God, that of thyne infinite goodnes, didest create our first parentes in the state of innocencye, wyth presente wealth and hope of heauen to come, til thorowe the diuels trayne their foly fel by synne to wrechednes, for thy tender pity of that passion that was payde for their and our redempcion, assist me so with thy gracious helpe, that vnto the subtil suggestions of the Serpent, I neuer so encline y eares of mine hart, but that my reason may resist them, & maister my sensualitp & refraine me from them.

More's second collect, as printed for the first time in his *English Works* (London, 1557).

3. GOD'S PLAN FOR THE RESTORATION OF MANKIND (p. 49)

O holy blessed Saviour Jesu[1] Christ, which willingly didst determine to die for man's sake, mollify mine hard heart, and supple it so by grace that, through tender compassion of thy bitter Passion, I may be partner of thine holy redemption.

---

[1] The Latin vocative *Jesu* (cf. the tenth and eleventh collects) had been adopted in medieval English, and spread at times to other cases : see it used also by Saint John Fisher at the end of this book.

4. BEFORE READING THE PASSION NARRATIVE (p. 52)

Good Lord, give us thy grace not to read or hear this gospel of thy bitter Passion with our eyen and our ears in manner of a pastime, but that it may with compassion so sink into our hearts that it may stretch to the everlasting profit of our souls.

5. THE PASCHAL LAMB AND THE EUCHARIST (p. 65-66)

Good Lord, which upon the sacrifice of the paschal lamb didst so clearly destroy the first-begotten children of the Egyptians that Pharaoh was thereby forced to let the children of Israel depart out of his bondage, I beseech thee, give me the grace in such faithful wise to receive the very sweet Paschal Lamb, the very blessed body of our sweet Saviour thy Son that, the first suggestions of sin by thy power killed in my heart, I may safe depart out of the danger of the most cruel Pharaoh, the devil.

Remember that *very* means *true* : the slain sheep is a shadow of the *real* Lamb of God.

6. THE GRACE OF DYING IN FAITH, HOPE AND LOVE (p. 68)

Good Lord, give me the grace so to spend my life that, when the day of my death shall come, though I feel pain in body, I may feel comfort in soul, and with faithful hope of thy mercy, in due love toward thee, and charity toward the world, I

may through thy grace depart hence into thy
glory.

Notice the first theological virtue in *faith-ful*, then two words
(*love* and *charity*) which define perfect *agapè*, and the positive
use of *world*, the world " the Father so loved that he gave his
only Son " (Jn 3.16). The connotation will be pejorative again in
collect n° 8.

7. CHRIST REJECTED BY THE SANHEDRIN (p. 75)

Gracious God, give me thy grace so to consider
the punishment of that false Great Council that
gathered together against thee that I be never, to
thy displeasure, partner nor give mine assent to
follow the sinful device of any wicked council.

The " punishment " refers to the destruction of Jerusalem
(A.D. 70) which brought the Jewish Sanhedrin to an end.

8. JUDAS' PRECEDENT DEPRECATED (p. 82)

O my sweet Saviour Christ, whom thine own
wicked disciple, entangled with the devil,
through vile wretched covetise betrayed, inspire, I beseech thee, the marvel of thy majesty,
with the love of thy goodness, so deep into
mine heart that, in respect of the least point of
thy pleasure, my mind may set alway this
whole wretched world at nought.

9. TO PRAY AWAY TEPIDITY (P. 85)

O my sweet Saviour Christ, which, of thine unde-
served love toward mankind, so kindly wouldst

suffer the painful death of the cross, suffer me not to be cold nor lukewarm in love-again toward thee.

10. THROUGH GOD'S LAW TO OUR HEAVENLY HOME (p. 100)

Almighty Jesu Christ, which wouldst for our example observe the law that thou camest to change, and being maker of the whole earth, wouldst have yet no dwelling house therein, give us thy grace so to keep thine holy law, and so to reckon ourselves for no dwellers but for pilgrims upon earth, that we may long and make haste, walking with faith in the way of virtuous works, to come to the glorious country wherein thou hast bought us inheritance for ever with thine own precious blood.

Allusions are clear to Lk 9.58 : " The Son of man hath not where to lay his head " (CW13/99), and to Heb 11.13-14 : " In what country soever we walk in this world, we be but as pilgrims and wayfaring men " (CW12/251).

11. LEARNING TO WASH EACH OTHER'S FEET (p. 117)

Almighty Jesu, my sweet Saviour Christ , which wouldst vouchsafe, [with] thine own almighty hands, to wash the feet of thy twelve apostles, not only of the good, but of the very traitor too, vouchsafe, good Lord, of thine excellent goodness, in such wise to wash the foul feet of mine affections, that I never have such pride enter into mine heart as to disdain, either in friend or foe, with meekness and charity for the love of thee, to [de]file mine hands with washing of their feet.

12. FOR A FRUITFUL SHARING IN THE EUCHARIST (p. 136)

Our most dear Saviour Christ, which, after the finishing of the old paschal sacrifice, hast instituted the new sacrament of thine own blessed Body and Blood for a memorial of thy bitter Passion, give us such true faith therein, and such fervent devotion thereto, that our souls may take fruitful ghostly food thereby.

Jesus said " Do this in memory of me " (Lk 22.19 and 1 Cor 11.24), a command quoted by More at least a dozen times. The *anamnesis* of today's eucharistic prayers explicitly commemorates Christ's death, and his rising from the dead, and (except for the Roman canon) his *parousia* or second coming in glory. Though More does quote " till he come " from 1 Cor 11.26, he finds, in that very passage, the accent to be on the Passion — Mass is a sacrifice — rather than on the Resurrection. All his books of 1534-35 link the Last Supper closely with the ensuing Passion. His short *Treatise to receive the Blessed Body* emphasises Saint Paul's urgent warning (1 Cor 11.27-29) against unexamined holy communion : a faithless communicant is " guilty of the body and blood of Our Lord " (*CW*13/194), he " eateth and drinketh judgment upon himself, in that he discerneth not the body of Our Lord " (*CW*13/196).

This crucifix is now among the More relics at Stony-hurst College, Lancashire, which is the heir of the Jesuit College at Saint-Omer, driven away by the French Revolution. Father Thomas More, S.J., gave it to the Sodality of Our Blessed Lady on 29 June 1755, with a document saying it had been used by his blessed ancestor. But the pearls would seem to fit it for a woman, and Lady Alice seems to be wearing it in Holbein's 1527 sketch of the More family. A Greek inscription on the reverse of the cross reads : " This is a relic of Thomas the Apostle ". It is described by Fr. Thomas Bridget in an appendix to his *Blessed Thomas More*, 2nd edition, (London, 1892), p. 456.

Our reproduction is taken from Professor Yvonne Hackenbroch's " Two relics of Sir Thomas More ", published in *The Connoisseur* of January 1977, p. 43.

A DEVOUT PRAYER

Thomas More's Last Prayer

The first printing of this text, in the edition of More's *English Works* by his nephew William Rastell (London, 1557), is introduced as follows :

> A devout prayer, made by Sir Thomas More knight, after he was condemned to die, and before he was put to death : who was condemned the Thursday the first day of July in the year of Our Lord God 1535, and in the 27th year of the reign of King Henry VIII, and was beheaded at the Tower Hill at London, the Tuesday following (CW13/228).

So this elaborate composition was the swan-song of the seasoned writer who had been sentenced to a traitor's death — dragging on hurdles to the gallows of Tyburn, unhanging while still alive, castrating, disembowelling, exhibiting of the head. It was penned in the shadow of impending death, yet also in the near-certainty of meeting execution with " faithful hope and charity " as " God's good servant ". It is structured along the traditional lines of liturgical prayer, with the *Pater, Ave, Credo* recited on the threshold, then a *mea culpa* to match the *Confiteor* which is recited at the beginning of the Mass and of Compline, then a universal bidding patterned on the suffrages that wind up the litany sung at Rogation time. Some Latin is left unenglished : More meant the prayer for his family circle, and given the circumstances could not contemplate the vast public it has reached ; his children knew Latin, and whoever acted as lector for a household was able to act as translator as well. The familiar echoes from the Latin Psalter and the Book of Hours will here be retained, and followed in brackets with the English equivalent, in More's own rendering whenever available.

Pater Noster. Ave Maria. Credo.

1. O holy Trinity, the Father, the Son, and the holy Ghost, three egal and co-eternal persons, and one almighty God, have mercy on me, vile, abject, abominable, sinful wretch, meekly acknowledging before thine high Majesty my long-continued sinful life, even from my very childhead hitherto. In my childhead, in this point and that point, etc. After my childhead, in this point and that point, etc, and so forth by every age.

2 Now, good gracious Lord, as thou givest me thy grace to acknowledge them, so give me thy grace, not in only word but in heart also with very sorrowful contrition to repent them, and utterly to forsake them. And forgive me those sins also, in which by mine own default, through evil affections and evil custom, my reason is with sensuality so blinded that I cannot discern them for sin. And illumine, good Lord, mine heart, and give me thy grace to know them, and to acknowledge them; and forgive me my sins negligently forgotten, and

bring them to my mind with grace to be purely confessed of them.

3. Glorious God, give me from henceforth the grace, with little respect unto the world, so to set and fix firmly mine heart upon thee, that I may say with thy blessed apostle Saint Paul : *Mundus mihi crucifixus est, et ego mundo. Mihi vivere Christus est, et mori lucrum. Cupio dissolvi et esse cum Christo.* [" The world is crucified to me, and I to the world " (Gal 6.14), " Christ is my life, and to die were mine advantage " (Phil 1.21, as rendered by More's grand-daughter in CW14/1086) ; " I long to be dissolved, that is to have my soul loosed and departed from my body, and to be with Christ " (Phil 1.23, in CW11/103)]

4. Give me the grace to amend my life, and to have an eye to mine end without grudge of death, which to them that die in thee, good Lord, is the gate of a wealthy life.

5. Almighty God, *Doce me facere voluntatem tuam. Fac me currere in odore unguentorum tuorum. Apprehende manum meam dexteram, et deduc me in via recta propter inimicos meos. Trahe me post te. In chamo et freno maxillas meas constringe, quum non approximo ad te.* [" Teach me to do thy will " (Ps 142.10). " Make me run in the odour of thy ointments " (Song of Songs 1.3). " Take me by the right hand, and lead me in thy way " (Ps 72.24, as englished by Mary Basset from More's Latin in CW14/1104) ; " *propter inimicos*, on account of [my] enemies " (Ps 26.11). " Draw me after thee " (Song 1.3). " With a snaffle and a bridle hold hard my jaws, o God,

when I do not approach toward thee " (Ps 31.9, in Mary Basset's version, CW14/1104)].

6. O glorious God, all sinful fear, all sinful sorrow and pensiveness, all sinful hope, all sinful mirth and gladness take from me. And on the other side, concerning such fear, such sorrow, such heaviness, such comfort, consolation and gladness as shall be profitable for my soul: *fac mecum secundum magnam bonitatem tuam, Domine.* [" Treat me according to your great goodness, Lord " (Ps 118.124)].

7. Good Lord, give me the grace, in all my fear and agony, to have recourse to that great fear and wonderful agony that thou, my sweet Saviour, hadst at the Mount of Olivet before thy most bitter passion, and in the meditation thereof, to conceive ghostly comfort and consolation profitable for my soul.

8. Almighty God, take from me all vainglorious minds, all appetites of mine own praise, all envy, covetise, gluttony, sloth, and lechery, all wrathful affections, all appetite of revenging, all desire or delight of other folks' harm, all pleasure in provoking any person to wrath and anger, all delight of exprobration or insultation against any person in their affliction and calamity.

9. And give me, good Lord, an humble, lowly, quiet, peaceable, patient, charitable, kind, tender and pitiful mind, with all my works, and all my words, and all my thoughts, to have a taste of thy holy, blessed Spirit.

10. Give me, good Lord, a full faith, a firm hope and a fervent charity, a love to thee, good Lord, incomparable above the love to myself; and that I love nothing to thy displeasure, but everything in an order to thee.

11. Give me, good Lord, a longing to be with thee, not for the avoiding of the calamities of this wretched world, nor so much for the avoiding of the pains of purgatory, nor of the pains of hell neither, nor so much for the attaining of the joys of heaven, in respect of mine own commodity, as even for a very love to thee.

    And bear me, good Lord, thy love and favour, which thing my love to thee-ward (were it never so great) could not but of thy great goodness deserve.

12. And pardon me, good Lord, that I am so bold to ask so high petitions, being so vile a sinful wretch, and so unworthy to attain the lowest. But yet, good Lord, such they be as I am bounden to wish, and should be nearer the effectual desire of them, if my manifold sins were not the let [impediment]. From which, O glorious Trinity, vouchsafe of thy goodness to wash me, with that blessed blood that issued out of thy tender body, O sweet Saviour Christ, in the divers torments of thy most bitter passion.

13. Take from me, good Lord, this lukewarm fashion, or rather key-cold manner of meditation, and this dullness in praying unto thee. And give me warmth, delight and quickness in thinking upon thee. And give me thy grace to long for thine holy sacraments, and specially to rejoice in the presence

of thy very blessed body, sweet Saviour Christ, in the holy sacrament of the altar, and duly to thank thee for thy gracious visitation therewith, and at that high memorial, with tender compassion, to remember and consider thy most bitter passion.

14. Make us all, good Lord, virtually participant of that holy sacrament this day, and every day make us all lively members, sweet Saviour Christ, of thine holy mystical body, thy Catholic Church.

15. *Dignare Domine die isto sine peccato nos custodire.*
Miserere nostri, Domine, miserere nostri.
Fiat misericordia tua, Domine, super nos, quemadmodum speravimus in te.
In te, Domine, speravi, non confundar in æternum.
Ora pro nobis, sancta Dei Genitrix, ut digni efficiamur promissionibus Christi.
[Vouchsafe, Lord, to keep us without sin this day. Have mercy upon us, O Lord, have mercy upon us (Ps 123.3). Let thy merciful kindness, O Lord, be upon us, like as we do put our trust in thee (Ps 32.22). In thee, O Lord, have I put my trust ; let me never be put to confusion (Ps 30.1 and 70.1). Pray for us, O holy Mother of God, that we may be made worthy of the promises of Christ].

Pro amicis

Almighty God, have mercy on N. and N. etc. (with special meditation and consideration of every friend, as godly affection and occasion requireth).

Pro inimicis

Almighty God, have mercy on N. and N. etc, and on all that bear me evil will, and would me harm; and their faults and mine together, by such easy, tender, merciful means as thine infinite wisdom best can devise, vouchsafe to amend and redress, and make us saved souls in heaven together, where we may ever live and love together with thee and thy blessed saints, O glorious Trinity, for the bitter passion of our sweet Saviour Christ. Amen.

Lord, give me patience in tribulation and grace in everything to conform my will to thine, that I may truly say : *Fiat voluntas tua, sicut in cælo et in terra.*

The things, good Lord, that I pray for, give my the grace to labour for. Amen.

NOTES TO THE PARAGRAPHS

1. O holy Trinity

Reviewing one's life through a systematic examination was no novelty : thus Saint Gertrude the Great, as quoted on her feastday (16 Nov.) in the breviary, revisits all the years *infantiæ et pueritiæ, adulescentiæ et iuventutis meæ* during which she offended God. The prayer for a special grace of discernment was inspired by Holy Writ, to witness this paragraph in *A Dialogue of Comfort* where More quotes two psalms (138.16 and 18.13) :

And some peradventure know not well their own affection themself..., and therefore saith the prophet unto God : " *Imperfectum meum viderunt oculi tui,* mine imperfection have thine eyen beholden " ; for which the prophet prayeth : " *Ab occultis meis*

> *munda me, Domine,* from mine hid sins cleanse thou
> me, good Lord " (CW12/226).

3. Glorious God

More's definition of *dissolvi* is matched, less fully, in Mary
Basset's translation of her grandfather : " I long to be dis-
charged of this body of mine " (CW14/1086). To be in that
mind comforted prisoner More, " for I can never but trust that
whoso long to be with Him shall be welcome to Him " (*Rogers*,
p. 537).

4. Give me the grace

More here incorporates into his prayer a sentence he had
read in a letter from his daughter Margaret (*Rogers*, p. 545).
Writing to her, he had himself praised " the wealthy [i.e.
happy] state of the life to come, for them that die in God. "
There is a clear echo of Apoc 14.13 : " Blessed are the dead who
die in the Lord ", cited by the liturgy in the service for the
dead.

7. Good Lord, give me the grace

This collect is almost a distillation of the *De Tristitia Christi,*
which More lacked time (and tools) to finish. It tallies with
various passages in his prison letters, for instance these lines to
Margaret : " I beseech him...give me grace and you both, in all
our agonies and troubles, devoutly to resort prostrate unto the
remembrance of that bitter agony which our Saviour suffered
before his passion at the Mount " (*Rogers*, p. 509). To his
daughter More suggests imitating the gesture of Jesus falling
flat, face on the ground, which he stresses repeatedly in
CW14/111-15, 147.

9. And give me, good Lord,

After listing the capital sins, More details, not the cardinal virtues, but rather the features of *agapè* according to 1 Cor 13, and the fruits of the Spirit according to Gal 5.23 : " charity, gladness, peace, patience, long-suffering, goodness, gentleness, faith, meekness, temperance " (CW8/757).

10. Give me, good Lord, a full faith,

More refers frequently to the three theological virtues ; Louis Martz finds them to provide the focus for the three books of *A Dialogue of Comfort* (Introduction to CW12). More sees them as the weapons of spiritual battle : " Let us fence us with faith, and comfort us with hope, and smite the devil in the face with a firebrand of charity " (CW12/318). The words " in an order to thee " are also found in John Fisher's famous " prayer for love ". The idea of an ordered love rested on Song of Songs 2.4 : *ordinavit in me caritatem*, which More's younger contemporary, Teresa of Avila, quotes five times as *Ordenó en mí la caridad*.

11. Give me, good Lord, a longing

" a longing to be with thee " echoes the *Cupio esse cum Christo* (Phil 1.23) quoted supra. The whole prayer for pure love parallels the famous 16th century sonnet *No me mueve, mi Dios, para quererte*.

14. Make us all, good Lord

The Eucharist, a major field in More's apologetic writings from 1532 to his incarceration, appeals to him as the sacrament of unity, at a time when the Anglican schism is rending that unity. We are *virtually* participant, that is we can reap the fruit, the *virtue* of the sacrament even when we do not — sometimes cannot, like Fisher and More in the Tower — corporally receive the Body of Christ : desire is enough. Its specific virtue is what the Creed calls " the communion of saints ", expressed in More's *Treatise on the Passion* as

> the unity or society of all good holy folk in the mystical body of Christ (CW13/142)... " We many be one bread and one body, as many as be partakers of one bread and one cup " (1 Cor 10.17, quoted p. 143)... It is also called, not only the sacrament of communion, but, over that, the *communion* itself, which is called in Latin *communio*, and *synaxis* in the Greek. And this blessed sacrament is called *the communion*, that is to say the union or gathering together in one, because that this sacrament doth not only signify that communion, but that the very real thing [=the true reality] that is in this blessed sacrament, beside the signification thereof, doth also effectually make it (p. 154). And so are we, as I say, by the receiving each of us that loaf that is Himself mystically, all incorporate together and all made that one loaf (p. 175). [Each communicant is] made a lively member in the pure mystical body, the fellowship and society of saints (176).

Here, as quite often in Scripture (e.g., Ps 149), especially in Saint Paul's greetings to his various churches (e.g., Rom 1.7 and 1 Cor 1.2), the *saints* are all the faithful (however imperfect) members of the Christian community.

15. Dignare Domine

Three of these Latin invocations hail from the Psalter, and by now you can tell that our translations are not by More : he would have said *good Lord*. We have used the version of the

Anglican *Book of Common Prayer*, the work of More's near-contemporary (and colleague since 1527), Thomas Cranmer. My copy is a gift from E.E. Reynolds, whose excellent biography, *The Field Is Won* (1968), owes much to the anthology he had compiled, *The Heart of Thomas More* (1966), including most of More's prayers.

If praise is not the leitmotiv of those prayers, it is because they belong to other genres, which More himself labels *meditations, suffrages, implorations*. But praise is 'understood' in the sense of *sous-entendu* : thus, here, the Latin verses constitute the tail-end of the *Te Deum laudamus*, which is pure praise. John Fisher recited the *Te Deum* just before he was beheaded, and when he came to *In te, Domine, speravi*, which is the beginning of Psalm 30, he went on with the psalm, complete with its sixth verse, *In manus tuas commendo spiritum meum* [" Into thy hands I commend my spirit "]. Now exegetes tell us that when Jesus spoke these words at the hour of his death (Lk 23.46), he had been praying its context as well, that is a psalm which breathes trust and confidence. Verse 15, " my hope hath been in thee, O Lord ; I have said, thou art my God ", ends with words which also occur in Psalm 15.2, *Deus meus es tu* : Pico, in his commentary, repeats them for emphasis ; More, who is apt to prune his model, does not do so here. The words *Deus meus es tu* (CW1/94.4, 95.27, 96.2, 9, 24), " my God thou art " (95.28), " my God art thou " (96.3, 10, 15, 16, 24-25 ; 97.15 and 21), occur thirteen times in Latin, eight in English. I have indicated the lines to show how intense is the use of this mantra.

We may now return to *In te, Domine, speravi*, which, as an incipit, is also the title of two psalms in Cranmer's *Common Prayer*, nos. 31 and 71 (30 and 70 in the Vulgate). In his *Imploratio*, More quotes the first 17 verses of Psalm 30, but skips the next two because they are imprecations against the unwrites *demones* in the margin, to make sure he does not pray *against* any fellow mortal : he seeks discomfiture only for mankind's immortal enemies. As for Psalm 70 (the other *In te, Domine, speravi*), More pauses at verse 18 (71.19 in the *Book of Common Prayer*) to write in the margin : *Gratias agit de liberatione a tribulatione vel tentatione*, " he gives thanks for being delivered from tribulation or temptation ".

The cover we reproduce was designed by Sister Madeleine du Calvaire, o.c.d., for *Moreana* 65-66 of June 1980, and re-used for nos. 70 and 73. Dürer's study for an apostle's hands (1508) is immensely popular even among non-Christians : it appeals to Far-Easterners, who make a similar gesture to greet fellow human beings. The Latin words are familiar to millions, since the *Book of Common Prayer* features them as the title of Psalm 31 and Psalm 71. They have been often quoted on memorial cards. They provide the motto carved above the gate of the castle of Droste zu Vischering (Westphalen), where the Blessed Maria do Divino Coração (d. Porto, 1899) saw the light of day. The double portcullis which connects More's Esses with the pendant alludes to the *castra* in Lancaster, but also to the many verses which describe God as a mighty fortress — an image exploited in Luther's *Ein feste Burg ist unser Herr* and Teresa's *Moradas del Castillo interior*.

The three inspired verses are followed by a prayer to Our Lady which was already traditional, and has remained so. It is recited before the concluding collect in the *Salve Regina*, the litanies of the Virgin, and the Angelus.

IN
TE

DOMI
NE
SPE
RAVI

TIME
TRIETH
TRVTH

MOREANA

BVLLETIN   THOMAS MORE

PUBLIÉ AVEC LE CONCOURS
DU C.N.R.S.

Pro inimicis

In More's English, your *friends* are all your dear ones, including kinsfolk. *Inimici* in the Psalter usually occurs with an imprecation : in the margin, More interprets the word, or other terms of hostility, as *diaboli* or *demones*, being loath to view any mortal as an enemy, and convinced that the worst enemies can do us more good than the closest friends (see § 35 of the prayer *Give me thy grace*). More looked forward to the heavenly company of not only the judges who had sentenced him to death, but even the king by whose order they were murdering him : he prays, on 5 March 1534, that " I should once meet with your Grace again in heaven, and there be merry with you " (*Rogers*, p. 490).

Fiat voluntas tua was even more proverbial than *In te, Domine, speravi*. More here quotes it from the *Pater noster*, but he has put it on the lips of Jesus, at times as *tua voluntas fiat*, while commenting on Mt 26.42 in his narrative of Christ's agony in Gethsemane.

The very last sentence of More's last prayer is also the most frequently quoted, and not seldom misquoted, though its success is due less to its message (" God helps those who help themselves " is proverbial in all languages), than to its pattern, two rhyming iambic hemistichs :

> The things, good Lord, that I pray for,
>
> Give me the grace to labour for.

PICO'S PRAYER TO GOD,

LORD AND FATHER

Giovanni Pico della Mirandola (1463-1494) crossed the sky of Quattrocento Italy like a brilliant meteor, and left a mass of writings, mostly in Latin, which his nephew Gianfrancesco gathered into a volume of *Opera Omnia* (1496), prefacing the book with a *Vita Ioannis Pici*. Early in life, perhaps around the time he chose to serve God in the married state, not as a priest, More compiled a selection consisting of that *Life*, an assortment of epistles and of ascetic rules, a commentary on Psalm 15 (*Conserva me*), and an *Elegia deprecatoria ad Deum*. He dedicated the *Life of John Picus* to a Poor Clare nun, " his right entirely beloved sister in Christ ", hoping to edify her and to " please any person that hath any mean desire and love to God " (CW1/51-52). Pico's epistles include some advice about how to pray, for instance the following exhortation in a letter to Gianfrancesco :

> When I stir thee to prayer, I stir thee not to the prayer which standeth in many words [Mt 6.7], but to that prayer which in the secret chamber of the mind, in the privy closet of the soul [Mt 6.6], with very affect [true feeling] speaketh to God, and in the most lightsome darkness of contemplation not only presenteth the mind to the Father, but also uni[t]eth it with him by unspeakable ways which

Title-page of More's *Life of Picus*
in the edition by Wynkyn de Worde

The keywords in the heading are *cunning* (which meant learning),
virtue and *wisdom*. The young man kneeling to the crucifix no doubt
represents Pico himself. The Passion of Christ is evoked by the sun
getting dark, the crown of thorns, the whips, the sponge, the soldier's
spear, even the cock whose crowing set Peter weeping for sorrow of
his cowardly denial.

only they know that have assayed. Nor I care not how long or how short thy prayer be, but how effectual, how ardent, and rather interrupted and broken-between with sighs than drawn on length with a continual row and number of words...What thou shalt in thy prayer ask of God, both the Holy Spirit which prayeth for us [cf. Rom 8.26], and eke [=also] thine own necessity shall every hour put in thy mind ; and also what thou shalt pray for, thou shalt find matter enough in the reading of Holy Scripture " (*CW1*/83-84).

The critical edition by Clarence H. Miller (Yale U.P., 1997) includes Pico's original Latin with a translation into modern English. The 84 lines (12 stanzas) which wind up the anthology will be found on pages 120-123 of *CW1*. Spelling and punctuation are here modernized, and the vowels which are muted or downtoned in today's speech are marked with an accent wherever they need stressing or at least sounding for the sake of rhyme or rhythm.

No work by Pico met with a greater success. It was translated into German by Jacob Wimpfeling, into French by two distinguished poets — the Catholic Joachim du Bellay and the Calvinist Louis des Masures — and even into Greek. The progress from servile dread to filial love is also advocated by Pico writing to his nephew : " Farewell, and love God, whom of old thou hast begun to fear " (*CW1*/93). The Christian soldier of his twelve rules and twelve weapons becomes the perfect lover whose " twelve properties or conditions " in *CW1*/113-120 immediately precede the closing prayer here reproduced.

1. O holy God of dreadful majesty,
    Verily one in three and three in one,
    Whom angels serve, whose work all creatures be,
    Which heaven and earth directest all alone,
    We thee beseech, good Lord[1], with woeful moan,
    Spare us wretches and wash away our guilt,
    That we be not by thy just anger spilt.

2. In strait balance of rigorous judgement
    If thou shouldest our sin ponder and weigh,
    Who able were to bear thy punishment ?[2]
    The whole engine of all this world, I say,
    The engine that enduren shall for aye,
    With such examination might not stand
    Space of a moment in thine angry hand.

3. Who is not born in sin original ?
    Who does not actual sin in sundry wise ?[3]
    But thou, good Lord, art he that sparest all[4],
    With piteous mercy tempering justice,
    For, as thou dost rewardes us devise
    Above our merit, so dost thou dispense
    Thy punishment far under our offence.

---

[1] *good Lord,* More's favourite vocative, occurs again in stanzas 3/3, 5/1 and 11/5, without any equivalent in Pico's Latin.

[2] Echoes the *De profundis* (Ps 129.3, and cf. Ps 142.2).

[3] Who does not commit actual sins in various ways.

[4] *parcis omnibus,* cf. Wisdom 11.27 and 12.16.

4. More[1] is thy mercy, far, than all our sin.
    To give them[2] also that unworthy be
    More godly is, and more mercy therein.
    Howbeit worthy enough are they, pardee,
    Be they never so unworthy, whom that he[3]
    List to accept which, wheresoever he taketh
    Whom he unworthy findeth, worthy maketh.

5. Wherefore, good Lord, that aye merciful art,
    Unto thy grace and sovereign dignity
    We silly[4] wretches cry with humble heart :
    Our sin forget and our malignity.
    With piteous eyes of thy benignity
    Friendly look on us once : thine own we be[5],
    Servants or sinners, whether it liketh thee[6].

---

[1] *More* is adjective, renders *major* (greater).

[2] *Them* bears the stress = even those.

[3] he...which = he who.

[4] *silly* (again in st. 12/2) means poor, pathetic, helpless.

[5] a biblical refrain ; we belong to God as our Maker and our Redeemer.

[6] whichever of those labels may please thee best.

6. Sinners, if thou our crime behold, certain [1] :
    Our crime, the work of our uncourteous[2] mind.
    But if thy giftès thou behold again,
    Thy giftès noble, wonderful and kind,
    Thou shalt us then the same personès find
    Which are to thee, and have be[en] longè space,
    Servants by nature, children by thy grace.

7. But this thy goodness wringeth[3] us, alas !
    For we whom grace had made thy children dear
    Are made thy guilty folk by our trespass :
    Sin hath us guilty made this many a year,
    But let thy grace, thy grace that hath no peer,
    Of our offense surmounten all the prease[4],
    That in our sin thine honour may increase.

---

[1] Chaucer very often uses *certain* as an adverb, meaning *certainly*, especially at the end of his lines : " Glad poverty is an honest thing, certain ", in *The Wife of Bath's Tale* (line 1183) is a good example, because young More, an avid reader of Chaucer, also praises the *glad poverty* of old philosophers such as Socrates, Diogenes, Democritus (CW1/38, line 202).

[2] Renders Pico's *ingratæ*, ungrateful, thankless.

[3] This goodness of yours weighs crushingly on us.

[4] *prease* : pressure, weight, from the French *presse*.

8. For though thy wisdom, though thy sovereign power
    May otherwise appear sufficiently,
    As thingès which thy creatures, every hour,
    All with one voice declare and testify,
    Thy goodness, yet, thy singular mercy,
    Thy piteous heart, thy gracious indulgènce,
    Nothing so clearly showeth as our offence.

9. What but our sin hath showed that mighty love
    Which able was thy dreadful majesty
    To draw down into earth fro[m] heaven above,
    And crucify God, that we, poor wretches we,
    Should from our filthy sin ycleansèd be
    With blood and water of thine owne side
    That streamèd from thy blessèd woundès wide[1].

10. Thy love and pity thus, o heavenly king,
    Our evil maketh matter of thy goodness :
    O love, o pity our wealth aye providing[2] !
    O goodness serving thy servants in distress !
    O love, o pity well-nigh now thankless !
    O goodness mighty, gracious and wise,
    And yet almost now vanquished with our vice !

---

[1] Jn 19.34 ; cf. More's *Treatise on the Passion* : " Out of the holy heart of Christ, when it was pierced with the spear, there issued both blood and water " (CW13/151.5-6, and cf. ib. p. 44.18-24).

[2] forever providing our happiness.

11. Grant, I thee pray, such heat into mine heart
    That to this love of thine may be egal [=equal].
    Grant me fro[m] Satan's service to astart [= escape],
    With whom me rueth[1] so long to have been thrall.
    Grant me, good Lord and creator of all,
    The flame to quench of all sinful desire,
    And in thy love set all mine heart afire ;

12. That, when the journey of this deadly life
    My silly ghost hath finishèd, and thence
    Departen must without his fleshly wife[2],
    Alone into his lordès high presènce,
    He may thee find, o well of indulgènce,
    In thy lordship not as a lord, but rather
    As a very tender-loving father[3]. Amen.

---

[1] *me rueth :* it grieves me (same root as *rueful*).

[2] The ghost, *spiritus* in Latin (the rational component of our nature), was seen as masculine ; the flesh, *caro* in Latin, was seen as feminine.

[3] More's 84 lines are not much longer than Pico's 61 hexameters, but he takes three lines to expand Pico's last line : *Non dominum sed te sentiat esse patrem.* More adds the epithet *very*, meaning *true*. Writing from prison to his family in 1534-35, More calls himself " your tender-loving father " (*Rogers*, pp. 507, 509, 559).

A SPURIOUS ATTRIBUTION

GIVE ME A GOOD DIGESTION, LORD

The peak year of the First World War, 1917, saw the appearance of two texts which have caught the fancy and the heart of our century. One, *Make me an instrument of your peace*, has become " *the* prayer " par excellence of Saint Francis, though it is anonymous and apocryphal. The other, *Give me a good digestion, Lord*, was composed by Thomas H.B. Webb, a Tommy who died in the field of honour on 1 December 1917, in his twentieth year. I consider its original to be the text on a plaque in the precincts of the cathedral of Chester, the author's parish. An article in *Moreana* 79-80 samples some of the variants that crept into the poem as it was reprinted in magazines or on bookmarks, translated into other languages, and even re-englished from those versions. The ascription to More owes much to the last stanza, begging for " a sense of humour " and " the power to see a joke " (or " the grace to see a joke ") : as *peace* suggests the paternity of the Assisi Poverello, *a sense of humour* suggests the English saint whom Francis Thompson hails as " Dear Jester in the courts of God ".

Give me a good digestion, Lord,
And also something to digest;
But when and how that something comes
I leave to Thee, Who knowest best.

Give me a healthy body, Lord;
Give me the sense to keep it so;
Also a heart that is not bored
Whatever work I have to do.

Give me a healthy mind, Good Lord,
That finds the good that dodges sight;
And seeing sin, is not appalled,
But seeks a way to put it right.

Give me a point of view, Good Lord,
Let me know what it is, and why.
Don't let me worry overmuch
About the thing that's known as " I ".

Give me a sense of humour, Lord,
Give me the power to see a joke,
To get some happiness from life
And pass it on to other folk.

PRAYING THROUGH

SAINT THOMAS MORE

Beatification in 1886 and canonization in 1935 gave More the official status of heavenly intercessor. Since 1970 he has been celebrated, jointly with Saint John Fisher, on 22 June, the date on which the bishop was martyred. The collect for their feast is :

> *Deus, qui veræ fidei formam in martyrio consummasti, concede propitius ut, sanctorum Ioannis et Thomæ intercessione roborati, fidem quam ore profitemur testimonio vitæ confirmemus.*

> [O God, who made martyrdom the highest expression of the true faith, grant, we beseech you, that strengthened by the intercession of Saints John and Thomas, we may bear witness through our life to the faith we profess with our lips.]

Before the Catholic liturgy was revised, in the wake of Vatican II, the collect had singled out " the defence of the supreme pontificate " as the cause for which these two martyrs shed their blood ; consequently the grace it prayed for was unity in the profession of that Catholic faith.

PRAYING TO SAINT THOMAS MORE

In a mass and office in their honour, the saints are evoked as models and mediators, rather than directly invoked. Yet More, " the patron of all in need " (Erasmus), " the best friend that the poor e'er had " (Shakespeare), has clients who address their requests to him as well as to heaven through him. The *alumni* of a school named for him in Philadelphia loved to sing at their reunion :

> May we, Saint Thomas More, pursue
> Thy golden march anew ;
> May we thy vict'ry flame renew
> And conquer heaven too.

More's name is not seldom part of the litany of the saints as sung at ordinations and religious professions. Ronald Knox composed a hymn in honour of Fisher and More, the last two stanzas being invocation. It ends as follows :

> To freedom and to wisdom friends,
> Look on a world unwisely free ;
> To bear the cross our Master sends,
> How slow, how frail, how faint are we !

By courtesy of Rev. Joseph B. Pierce, the photographer, you see here a statue made in Italy, and erected by Msgr. William J. Awalt in the Church of St. Joseph on Capitol Hill, Washington, to inspire the lawyers, judges and legislators who work at the US Senate or the Supreme Court, both located in the parish. The text has much in common with " A Lawyer's Prayer ", quite familiar to the Thomas More Societies of North America. We quote the first two and the last paragraphs :

Thomas More, counselor and advocate, learned in the law, chancellor of charity and jurist of justice, merry martyr, scholar and canonized saint, may the Lord of all law and of all lawyers make me at your request a little more like you today than I was yesterday.

Pray that for the greater glory of God and in pursuit of His justice, I may be able in argument, accurate in analysis, strict in study, correct in conclusion, candid with clients, honest with adversaries, faithful in all details to the faith. Sit with me at my desk and listen with me to my client's tales. Read with me in my library and stand beside me in court so that today I shall not, to win a point, lose my soul.

Lord Chancellor, stand retained by us before the Infinite Lord Justice who will preside when we are to be tried.

Under a portrait of More given me by Dr. Marie-Louise Johnson at Yale in 1961, there are five paragraphs. Here are the first two :

St. Thomas More, be our advocate and counsel before the Divine tribunal that alone is without error.

Bespeak for us the wisdom to apply the precepts of God's eternal law to the problems of our daily practice.

On Lady Day 1973, to greet the triple volume of More's *Confutation* (at last out of press), Ph. D. candidate Robert B. Shaw sent these lines to Richard Sylvester, Executive Editor of *The Complete Works of St. Thomas More* :

To Saint Thomas More

Defender of the Faith from its Defender[1],
Bearing consistent witness to the last,
What homages our scholarship can render
Sit dimly on you at the Lamb's repast.
Yet when, to later days, your scribes restore
The exploits of a mind precise and vast
In volumes each proclaiming how you wore
Your chain of Esses, we discern a splendor
Bidding us read, look up, and pray for **More**.

The young academic writer knows that the canonized martyr need not be prayed for, what he seeks is more of More, both the person and his works. The jacket of all the volumes of *CW* reproduces the Esses, (S has been interpreted as SERVANT), the Lancaster portcullis (which does duty as a clasp) and the heraldic Tudor rose, sung by More in a poem about the coalescence of the two rival Roses (*CW*1/116).

---

[1] Henry VIII

In 1974, Peter Steele, S.J., on More's feast-day, in the chapel of St. Thomas More College, near Perth (Australia), read a poem from which we quote twenty lines :

> I used to think of you as a figure of style,
>   who poised himself with the others for Holbein :
> a wit as sharp as God could want, and as blunt
>   as the king could bear : a martyr caught
> at the edge of death, unable to break the habit
>   of making jokes : amused and English,
> performing homage to heaven not from a pulpit,
>   but in a theatre of the absurd.
>
> Perhaps. But now, though Henry is gone to his place,
>   the wrath of the king is still death : and now
> that Utopia lingers, just as you guessed, nowhere
>   and everywhere : now that children debate
> the acting of Scofield, but cannot imagine the point
>   of the prayers in the dark,[1] I return to your image,
> hardy thinker, gentle speaker, courtier
>   of life, a humanist to the death.
>   Old friend,
>   think of me often, speak of me with God.

Leaving aside other poems, in various languages, especially German and Spanish, which are scattered throughout *Moreana* and the *Thomas More Gazette,* we end with an ode which Francis Thompson, in 1905, was commissioned to write in honour of the English martyrs. More heads the procession with 28 lines. We quote the first seven :

---

[1] In Fred Zinnemann's oscar-winning film of 1966, not only does More pray (too briefly) with his wife Alice and Margaret, but he kneels in silent prayer before entering Westminster Hall for his trial.

> Ah, happy Fool of Christ ! unawed
> By familiar sanctities,
> You served your Lord at holy ease.
> Dear Jester in the Courts of God
> In whose spirit, enchanting yet,
> Wisdom and love together met,
> Laughed on each other for content !

Thompson took More for his lodestar both as artist and as Christian man. One of his last poems ends with this wonderful appeal :

> Thomas More,
> Teach (thereof my need is sore)
> What thou showedst well on earth —
> Good writ, good wit, make goodly mirth !

" Surely the last line could provide an appropriate 'motto' for Thomas More's *amici* of today ", writes Brigid Boardman, who edited both poems in *Moreana* 101-102/87-92.

Moreana n°1/62 (September 1963) suggests a brief invocation which alludes to the scene where Elisha, to obey Elijah's request of a share in his spirit, dropped his mantle for him to wear as a symbolic heirloom (2 Kings 2.9-13). The prayer is a half line spoken at Agincourt by the king addressing the old 'white-headed' knight Sir Thomas Erpingham : " Lend me thy cloak, Sir Thomas ! " (*Henry V*, Act IV, scene 1).

This Vatican stamp issued on 7 May 1985 reproduces a 1629 Cologne edition designed by Antonello Ciaburro.

SAINT JOHN FISHER

PRAYER FOR THE SPIRIT OF LOVE

On 14 June 1535, More's last interrogatory focused on his correspondence with John Fisher. That they had used similar terms in their refusal of the schismatic oaths, More ascribed to "the conformity of our wits [=minds], learning and study ". Such was the conformity of their souls that a prayer written by the bishop of Rochester (*Johannes Roffensis*) was published under More's name, in 1937, by A. G. Dickens, who had found it among the papers of a Yorkshire curate as being More's. Later on, it was discovered on five pages in Fisher's hand, with erasures and additions (often interlinear) which could only be authorial. The text we offer is closer to the autograph than the one appended by E. E. Reynolds to his *St. John Fisher* of 1972, and by Jean Rouschausse, in French, at the end of his 1964 anthology. Fisher's Latin *Treatise of Prayer*, translated into English, was printed at Paris in 1630 for the Catholic Recusants, and again in 1887 at London and New York. *Moreana* n° 89 reproduces his seven short invocations to Jesus, one for each day of the week : for Sunday, it is " O blessed Jesu, make me to love thee entirely ! " ; for Saturday, " O sweet Jesu, possess my heart, hold and keep it only to thee ! "

Help me, most loving Father, help me with thy mighty grace. Succour me with thy most gracious favour. Rescue me from these manifold perils that I am in, for unless thou wilt of thy infinite goodness relieve me, I am but as a lost creature.

Thy strait [=strict] commandment is that I should love thee with all my heart, with all my soul, with all my mind, with all my power. And this, wot [=know] I well, I do not, but am full far short and wide therefrom ; which thing I perceive by the other loves that I have had of thy creatures heretofore. For such as I sincerely loved, I loved them so that I did seldom forget them. They were ever in my remembrance and almost continually mine heart was occupied with them and my thought ever ran upon them as well absent as present. Specially when they were absent I much desired to have their presence and to be there where they were, or else my heart were never in any restful quiet.

But alas, my dear Father, I am not in this condition towards thee. For I keep not thee in my remembrance, nor bear thee in my thought, nor occupy my heart with thee so oft as I should, but for every trifle that cometh to my mind I let thee slip and fall out thereof, and for every fantasy that stirreth my heart I set thee aside and shortly forget thee.

I suffer many a trifling thought to abuse my soul at liberty, but with thee, my dear Father, have I lightly done, and forthwith turn me to the remembrance of thy creatures and so tarry with thee but a short while. The delight of thy creatures so pulleth me and draweth me hither and thither, my wretched desires so blind me, the false world so deceiveth me that I forget thee, that art my most loving Father and art so much desirous to have my heart and love. What are thy creatures but creatures made by thee ? Thou madest me and them of naught, and thou far incomparably passest all them. And what are my desires, when they are set upon thy creatures and not in an order to thee ?.... If it so were I loved thee with all my heart, I should long to have a sight of thy most blessed face, I should earnestly desire to see thy joyous country and kingdom, I should ever covet to be there present with thee and thy most glorious court.

But this, alas, I do not. And therefore I sorrow at my grievous negligence, I weep for my damnable forgetfulness, I lament my foolishness, yea, my very madness, that thus for trifles and vanities forget my most dear and loving Father. Alas, woe is me ! What shall I do ? Whither may I turn me ? To whom shall I resort for help ? Where shall I seek for a remedy against this worldly and earthly dullwardness of my heart ? Whither should I rather go than to my Father, to my most loving Father, to my most merciful Father, to him that of his infinite love and mercy hath given me boldness to call him Father ? Whose son Jesu my Saviour hath taught me thus to call him, and to think verily that he is my Father, yea, and a more loving Father than is any natural father unto his child. These are his words spoken unto the natural fathers of this world : " When ye that are infect with evil can liberally give unto your children good gifts, how much rather your heavenly Father shall give a good spirit to them that ask it of him ? " [Mt 7.11].

These words, most gracious Father, are the words of thy most dearly beloved son, Jesu, wherein he teaches us that thou art our very Father and maketh promise on thy behalf that thou shalt give thine holy spirit unto them that ask it of thee studiously. Thou wilt that we should believe him and faithfully trust his words. For thou testifiedst of him that he was thine entirely beloved son and badest us hear him and give a full faith unto his words. Wherefore we may be certain and sure of three things : the first, that thou art our Father ; the second, that thou art a more loving Father unto us than are the carnal fathers of this world unto their children ; the third, that thou wilt give, to such as devoutly ask it of thee, thy most holy Spirit. We may be well assured that for thine inestimable goodness, and for the honour of thy name and thy everlasting truth, thou wilt not disappoint thy promises, forasmuch as they were made by thy most entirely beloved son Christ Jesu, whom thou sentest into this world to make the truth certain and to confirm the same unto us by his most precious blood, which he shed for us upon the cross.

O Father, then, where shall I rather seek for help in my necessity than at thee which wilt have me call thee by this name ? a name of much love and tenderness, of much delight and pleasure, a name which stirreth the heart to much hope and comfort, and to many other delectable affections. And if nothing were told me but only this name, it might suffice to make me steadfastly trust that thou, which hast commanded me to call thee by this name Father, wilt help me and succour me at my need whensoever I sue unto thee ; but much rather because my Saviour thy son Christ Jesu hath assured me that thou art a more kind and more loving Father unto me than was mine own natural father. This assurance made by thy most entirely beloved son should specially move both thee and me. First it should move me to have an hope and a confidence that thou wilt deal with me according to the same promise. Secondly, it should also move thee to perform this promise effectually and so to show thyself a kind and loving Father. This my petition, most dear Father, is agreeable to that same promise made by thy most entirely beloved son, my Saviour Jesu. I ask none other thing but thy good and holy Spirit, which he promised to be given unto all that ask it.

I know, most gracious Father, that thou art here present with me albeit I see thee not. But thou both seest me and hearest me and no secret of my heart is hid from thee. Thou hearest that I now ask thine holy Spirit and thou knowest that I now pray therefor and that I am very desirous to have the same. O dear Father, with all the enforcement of my heart I beseech thee to give thine holy Spirit unto me. Wherefore, unless thou wilt disappoint the promise of thy son Jesu, thou canst not but give me this holy Spirit, so that I may be fully relieved of that misery whereof I complained unto thy goodness before. Thy most holy Spirit he shall make me to love thee with all my heart, with all my soul, with all my mind, with all my power, for he is the author of all good love, he is the very furnace of charity, he is the very fountain of all gracious affections and godly desires. He is the spiritual fire that kindleth in the heart of them where he entereth all gracious love ; he filleth their souls in whom he is received with the abundance of charity ; he maketh their minds sweetly to burn in all godly desires and giveth unto them strength and power courageously to follow all ghostly affections, and specially towards thee.

Wherefore, dear Father, when thou hast straitly [=strictly] commanded me thus to love thee with all my heart, and thus would I right gladly do (but without thy help and without thy holy Spirit I cannot perform the same), I beseech thee to shed upon my heart thy most holy Spirit, by whose gracious presence I may be warmed, heated and kindled with the spiritual fire of charity, and with the sweetly burning love of all godly affections, that I may fastly set my heart, soul and mind upon thee, and assuredly trust that thou art my very loving Father and, according to the same trust, I may love thee with all my heart, with all my soul, with all my mind and with all my power. Amen.

Dame Alice More by Holbein, wearing the crucifix which we encountered on p. 56 and reading from her *Prayer Book*.

LANDMARKS IN MORE'S LIFE

1474.   John More of London marries Agnes Granger.

1477 or 1478. Birth of their second child and eldest son Thomas, " on Friday after the feast of the Purification of the Blessed Virgin Mary ", or Candlemas (2 February). Exact day and year remain uncertain.

1494.   Leaves Oxford to begin common law in London.

1496.   Enters his father's legal college, Lincoln's Inn (12 February).

1499.   Erasmus' first of 7 visits to England : befriends More.

1501.   Utter barrister ; as guest of the London Carthusians, examines his vocation to the priesthood.

1504.   Weds Joanna Colt, who gives him 4 children.

1509.   Henry VIII (d. 1547) succeeds his father as king.

1510-1518.   More serves the City as Undersheriff.

1511.   On Joanna's death, he marries Alice Middleton.

1515.   First embassy. *Utopia* begun in Antwerp.

1516.   Editio princeps of *Utopia* at Louvain.

1517-1518.   After second embassy, drawn into royal service.

1521.   Created knight (hence *Sir* Thomas) and Undertreasurer.

1523.   Speaker of the House of Commons. Defends Henry VIII's *Assertio* against Luther.

1524.   Chancellor of the royal duchy of Lancaster.

1528.   Begins writing in English against heretics.

1529.   Succeeds Cardinal Wolsey as Lord Chancellor (25 October).

1532.   Resigns the Chancellorship (16 May)

1534.   Imprisoned for refusing to sign the Act of Succession (17 April).

1535.   Beheaded for high treason (6 July).

AND AFTERLIFE

1557. His *English Works* appear in London under Mary Tudor.

1565. His *Opera Latina* are published in Louvain.

1588. Stapleton's *Vita Thomæ Mori* (Douai*)*.

1593. The Elizabethan stage censor vetoes the play *Sir Thomas More*.

1886. Leo XIII officializes the cult rendered to 54 English martyrs, Fisher and More heading the list.

1927. First volume of a planned edition of More's works (London).

1935. Pius XI canonizes John Fisher and Thomas More (19 May).

1960. Robert Bolt's *A Man for All Seasons* (London).

1961. First book issued at Yale U. by the More Project : *Selected Letters*.

1962. Foundation of *Amici Thomæ Mori* (Brussels, 29 December).

1966. Fred Zinnemann's oscar winning film *A Man for All Seasons* (Hollywood).

1969. Public statue by Cubitt Bevis (Chelsea).

1970. Paul VI places John Fisher and Thomas More on the universal calendar, with a joint feast on 22 June.

Thomas More Symposium at St John's University, on Utopia Parkway (New York).

1977-1978. Thomas More Exhibition at the National Portrait Gallery, various Quincentennial Congresses, and reprint of the *English Works*.

1981. First *Thomas-Morus-Jahrbuch* (Düsseldorf).

1985. Fisher and More Congress (Chelsea and London) to celebrate the Golden Jubilee of their canonization.

1989. More Symposium at St. Thomas More College, Saskatoon, Canada.

1992. " New Worlds and Utopia " Conference of the *Amici Thomæ Mori* at Sydney, Australia.

1995. Conference at Mainz, Germany, on " Europe as Cradle of Humanism and the Reformation ".

1998. Conference at Maynooth College, Ireland, on " Thomas More in His Time : Renaissance Humanism and Renaissance Law ".

BIBLIOGRAPHY

The Complete Works of St. Thomas More (Yale. : *CW* with volume number).

CW 1   English Poems. Life of Pico. The Last Things.
CW 2   Richard III (English and Latin).
CW 3   Part I : Lucian Translations. Part II : Latin Poems.
CW 4   *Utopia.*
CW 5   *Responsio ad Lutherum* (in two parts).
CW 6   Dialogue concerning Heresies (in two parts).
CW 7   Letter to Bugenhagen. Supplication of Souls. Letter against Frith.
CW 8   Confutation of Tyndale's Answer (in three parts).
CW 9   Apology of Sir Thomas More.
CW 10   Debellation of Salem and Byzance.
CW 11   Answer to a Poisoned Book.
CW 12   Dialogue of Comfort against Tribulation
CW 13   Treatise upon the Passion. Treatise upon the Blessed Body. Instructions and Prayers.
CW 14   *De Tristitia Christi* (in two parts).
CW 15   In Defence of Humanism.

Editions in modernized spelling, in both hardback and paperback, have been published by Yale for : Selected Letters, Utopia, Richard III with selection of poems, Tower Works (from *CW*13), A Dialogue of Comfort, The Sadness of Christ (from *CW*14).

Biographies abound, with only two having, over the decades, achieved the status of classics : T.E. Bridgett, *The Blessed Thomas More* (London, 1891), R.W. Chambers, *Thomas More* (London, 1935). The article " Thomas More, Sir/Saint " in *Encyclopædia Britannica*, first published in 1974, was updated in 1997 toward its electronic edition.

No biography will bring people's personalities to life so well as their writings : the only serious gap remaining in More sources is an edition of the letters not included in the Yale *CW*, especially those of his last two years, 1534-1535. The latest and fullest anthology, *Sir Thomas More Reader : Tales and Anecdotes from the English Writings*, edited by Rudolph E. Habenicht, revised edition 1998, is available in paperback for US $ 22 postage included, from Chelsea Press, P.O. Box 684, Naalehu, H1 96772, USA.